D0824119

How to Help a
Heartbroken Friend

Also by David B. Biebel

Jonathan, You Left too Soon

If God Is So Good, Why Do I Hurt So Bad?

How to Help a Heartbroken Friend

What to Do and What to Say When a Friend Is Going through Tough Times

by David B. Biebel, D.Min.

Revised Edition

Hope Publishing House
Pasadena, California

Copyright © 2004 David B. Biebel
Revised Edition

All rights reserved.

**Previously published in 1993 by Thomas Nelson, Inc.
and in 1995 by Fleming H. Revell's New Spire.**

For information address:

Hope Publishing House
P.O. Box 60008
Pasadena, CA 91116 - U.S.A.
Tel: (626) 792-6123 / Fax: (626) 792-2121
E-mail: hopepub@sbcglobal.net
Web site: http://www.hope-pub.com

Printed on acid-free paper
Cover design — Michael McClary/The Workshop

Library of Congress Cataloging-in-Publication Data

Biebel, David B.
  How to help a heartbroken friend : what to do and what to say
when a friend is going through tough times / by David B. Biebel.--
Rev. ed.
      p. cm.
  ISBN 1-932717-01-3 (trade pbk. : alk. paper)
  1. Caring--Religious aspects--Christianity. 2. Helping behavior--
Religious aspects--Christianity. 3. Friendship--Religious aspects--Chris-
tianity. I. Title.
  BV4647.S9B54 2004
  253--dc22

                                                        2004001552

Foreword

The spirit of the Lord God is upon me,
    because the Lord has anointed me;
    he has sent me to bring good news to the oppressed,
       to bind up the brokenhearted,
    to proclaim liberty to the captives,
       and release to the prisoners;
    to proclaim the year of the Lord's favor,
       and the day of vengeance of our God;
       to comfort all who mourn;...
       to give them a garland instead of ashes,
    the oil of gladness instead of mourning,
       the mantle of praise instead of a faint spirit.
They will be called oaks of righteousness,
    the planting of the Lord, to display his glory.
They shall build up the ancient ruins,
       they shall raise up the former devastations;
    they shall repair the ruined cities,
       the devastation of many generations.

—Isaiah 61:1-4

For Ilona

Author's Notes

Revised edition

UNLESS OTHERWISE INDICATED or obvious from the text, the stories in this book are based on the true experiences of people who know about heartbreak and its physical, relational, psychic and spiritual pain. To each of these, my fellow pilgrims, I wish a personalized overflowing portion of God's grace. Except for autobiographical anecdotes, I have disguised identities and altered some details in order to protect the privacy of individuals involved. Any remaining similarity to any person other than myself is not intentional.

Contents

1

What to say when you don't know what to say

Sometimes nothing is best.

AFTER THREE YEARS of faithful service to an aerospace corporation, Marty lost his job. He went to work one day and, in between the classes he was teaching, he heard the rumor. Two weeks later it was confirmed by a terse note that sent the 47-year-old human relations expert reeling: *We regret that due to an unforeseen downturn in our markets worldwide, your position has been terminated.*

The initial shock was tough enough. Worse, though, was that after four months of trying everywhere and everyone he knew, Marty still had no job. Not even a prospect of a job. What had started as a challenge had slowly ground away his confidence and self-respect to the point where life seemed pointless and he even considered suicide as a solution.

Finally, one day, the frustration and fears got the best of him. Alone in his apartment, Marty started shouting at God, "Why did you do this to me? What did I do to deserve this?

Don't you care what happens to me?" The heartbroken man carried on for some time, venting his anger, screaming and pounding on things.

After there were no more tears to cry, he noticed his dog, Mandy, cowering behind the living room chair, a witness to the whole thing. "Come here, pup," Marty said quietly as he sat down to recover his composure. "You should be glad you're a dog. At least you can't get fired from being man's best friend." Then Marty explained to Mandy just how tough things had become lately.

When he was done, he took the dog out for a walk, partly to be sure nobody else in the condo had overheard the tantrum. Thankfully, nobody had – or if so, they didn't let on. Relieved at this, Marty was even more relieved to have gotten the bitterness out of his system.

You might think the relief came from all the things he said to God, and certainly that was part of it. But Mandy played a big part, too. Unlike some of Marty's human friends, his faithful dog didn't argue or offer solutions or advice. She just listened, wagging her tail and licking her master's hand once in awhile to let him know she cared.

Let's face it. Life hurts. Sometimes it hurts so bad it seems that nothing could ease the pain, much less heal the wound causing the distress. This is as true for Bible-believing, church-going, born-again people as it is for everybody else. In fact, your brokenhearted Christian friends may have it worse because, like Marty, they have to deal with whatever loss has occurred while wondering, *Where was God when I needed God?*

Before you rush to offer a dispassionate, logical or even *theo*logical answer to this question, remember Mandy. If you rush to fix what's broken – broken *hearts* are the ultimate challenge – you may miss the point completely. Marty simply needed somebody to hear him out, a sounding board, someone willing to enter his pain and share it with him. When the crisis came to a head, Mandy's compassionate presence was more comforting to Marty than all the suggestions made by his pastor and church friends, who seemed either unable to understand or unwilling to authenticate his suffering.

The reason I begin with Marty's story – instead of one of the more horrific tales you'll hear about shortly – is to illustrate something crucial about heartbreak. The intensity of Marty's grief had more to do with his background and personality than with the relative magnitude of his loss. The human "help" he had received was meaningless, at best, and infuriating, at worst, because it failed to connect with Marty uniquely, individually, right where he was, without judging him for being there and without telling him how he should feel or what he should do to get out.

The Continuum

Now let's go to your church together and try to identify the brokenhearted people in the pews around us. They're not usually easy to find, because they arrived all prissied up and bravely masked to match everybody else. But look into their eyes, observe the stress in their faces and the tension in their frames. If your church allows opportunities for people to express themselves, listen to the meaning – really, a yearning – hidden in what they ask or say. It's a simple longing: *Won't somebody please just be my friend?*

You may not be able to pick up these vibes without some practice. But for the sake of the 30 percent (my estimate may be much too low) of the people around you in any church service who fit this category, I hope you won't give up too easily.

Contrary to what you may believe, you don't have to endure some disaster before you can bring a touch of God's grace to a heartbroken friend. If I might rephrase the apostle Paul: "Shall we hurt the more that grace may the more abound? May it never be!" In 2 Corinthians 1 Paul reminds us that we've all had pain of some kind, and with God's help we can comfort others with the same kind of comfort we received from God.

Comfort, like pain, is a continuum. It's true that widows understand widows, but it's not true that you have to be a widow to help one of them toward wholeness. In fact, sometimes a potential comforter's previous loss may hinder her ability to really help a heartbroken friend if the helper has not yet resolved her own issues. When this is true, the helper may try to work out her own pain through the other person, which is neither fair nor helpful because while the "comforter" may feel better as a result, the heartbroken person will end up more confused.

But anyone willing to walk in a heartbroken friend's shoes for awhile can be helpful, even if her greatest tragedy to date was getting dumped for somebody else as an adolescent. You can make all the difference in a friend's healing.

Lonely Even in a Crowd

Our hypothetical church service has gotten beyond the announcements, hymns, special music and the offering, but you still haven't zeroed in on anybody who seems to exhibit more than normal distress. So we might as well listen to what the guest speaker is saying.

"Listen, grump," he says. "You know what your problem is? Your attitude! Life has its problems. We all know that. Nobody said it would be easy, but why all the doom and gloom? Everybody falls into a pit once in awhile, but you don't have to wallow in it, throwing a pity party nobody wants to attend. We're not pigs ... we're eagles, who on wings of faith can rise above anything and everything the devil throws our way.

"Did you wake up this morning with a chip on your shoulder? Then get back in that bed and get out on the other side! Happiness is a choice, after all. If you're depressed, it's because you *want* to be depressed. Maybe you even *like* to be depressed. If you can't see the bright side of life, it's because you don't *want* to. There's no other logical – or spiritual – reason.

"You've got to take off those melancholy spectacles and look at life with positive eyes of faith! God gave you two eyes for a reason. Some people gaze at their problem with both eyes and never look at God. Some gaze at the problem with one eye and glance at God with the other. Some glance at the problem with one eye and gaze at God with the other. But the only way to live the victorious life is to gaze at God with both eyes, and never give those little problems the slightest glance."

As the preacher launches into another entertaining story to support his point, you notice that Nancy, just to your right and one pew forward – almost within reach – is weeping silently, with a slightly bowed head. You might be surprised to know that the most alone she ever feels is when she's in church. If you earn the right to get inside her pain, you'll find out why.

Nancy attends your church every week, not out of obligation or as a social event, and certainly not to be entertained. She keeps coming because in her heart of hearts she is still a little girl who believes that her heavenly Father loves her more than she dares to ask or think. That child-like faith kept her sane when her older brother tortured her by leaving her on a blanket under which numerous mousetraps had been set. Her caring Father was there in her hiding place, a hollow in the stream bank behind her home. And when she began splitting into different personalities to mentally escape the more extreme abuses that came later, God loved each "person" in a slightly different way.

When Nancy goes to church, she sees – and is frightened by – the mass of people. She hears about all the programs and plans, and like everyone else she stands up and sits down on cue. She gives what she can and she tries to stay open to the sermons, although the one she's hearing right now and others like it only add to her overwhelming sense of shame, while increasing her fear that nobody really understands or cares. She told me once she's been to a lot of churches, but almost everywhere she goes she feels like an alien, disconnected from everybody else.

More than anything, Nancy desperately needs—and wants—to stay in touch with the ever-healing Spirit of God. The good news is, you can help. The bad news is, getting involved with her will cost you—time, energy, but mostly love. She doesn't need another program, even a small-group program. She's endured a lot of them already. She doesn't need a psychiatrist. She's seen dozens of them already, and one has made himself available by phone, anytime.

What Nancy really needs is a friend. One will do.

People Can Say the Stupidest Things

Nancy's sense of disconnection may be more extreme than most, but its one of heartbreak's common themes. And one of the reasons is the frequency of dialogues like the following hypothetical conversation between Martha (M), a new widow, and Katherine (K), who has come to "comfort" her:

K: I don't have to pick up the kids for 20 minutes, so I just thought I would stop in and comfort you, like Jesus said.

M: I'm so glad you came over. I just feel so isolated, and so...

K: But honey, Jesus is with you.

M: I know Jesus is with me.

K: He said he'll never leave us. Your husband left you, but Jesus said that *he'll* never leave you.

M: Well, I still was feeling really lonely, and I apprec—

K: I know just how you feel. This happened to my mother-in-law. When her first husband died, she was just beside herself. We didn't know what to do with her. But then she started going to another church and she met this nice widower. I'm sure that the Lord in his time will bring you another mate.

M: I'm really not interested in another mate.

K: She said the very same thing!

M: Do you really think there's something wrong with me that

I'm feeling lost and lonely? I know Jesus is here with me and I find comfort in the Scriptures, but I still miss my husband.

K: Oh, Martha, but he's in heaven. He wouldn't want to come back here even for ten minutes because he's with the Lord. You wouldn't want to wish him back in this wicked world.

M: Well, what about me?

K: Now I've never lost a husband, but I know that time takes care of things like this.

M: How can you know that if you've never experienced it?

K: I just read the Word. I just believe what God says.

M: (to herself: *Haven't you ever read the book of Job?*) I appreciate your coming, and I appreciate what you've had to say, and I welcome company anytime. I'll see if there's something wrong with me that I feel the way I do.

K: Well, you just keep praying. And call me anytime. I'm happy to come over and be God's comfort.

M: Any time I need your comfort, I'll call....

It'll be a hot day at the North Pole before Martha calls Katherine to come and "comfort" her again. But Katherine will probably expect that call. Not only that, she may be offended not to hear from Martha, now that she's gone out of her way to minister to Martha's need. To top it off, she may even chastise Martha, probably in the church foyer or parking lot, for not calling and for the way she has withdrawn from people, when a lot of women have had it worse than her.

Actually, in this interchange, Martha was more confrontational with Katherine than most heartbroken people dare or care to be, either because they don't have the energy or because they're too emotionally numb to get angry. If there's anything that comes through loud and clear from my research into this question, it's this: For some reason people who want to help often aren't wise enough to say nothing when they don't know what to say.

The Sounds of Silence

Perhaps to defend God's honor, or to try to make some sense of what has happened or simply to put the whole thing in the past, most would-be comforters are convinced that *something must be said.* That was Marty's experience when what he really needed was somebody to let him unload. In other words, his friends might have communicated more by not saying anything.

When the eleven-year-old brother of a personal friend died, after the funeral and the reception and just about the time everybody was leaving, the pastor showed up at the family's home. He took a seat in the living room and sat there for a couple of hours, listening, observing, just being around. After the well-wishers had left, he still stayed for awhile. Then he talked a little with the family, prayed with them and left. The net impact: *Dallas came. Dallas was here.* That was what they remembered after the flowers wilted and the hoopla died away.

Being there is more important than almost anything else. I learned this myself in the spring of 1979, sitting on the bank of a small pond in the little town in Michigan's Upper Peninsula where I was the only pastor. A young boy had drowned and as I sat with his mother on that hillside waiting for the diver to find the boy's body, I didn't know what to say, so I didn't say much.

But this brokenhearted mother knew I cared and maybe she thought I understood, having buried my own three-year-old son Jonathan the previous fall. As we waited, being there was all I could offer. Sometimes it's the best and only way to deal with a hurt that pious words of consolation might only magnify.

Since you're reading this book, it's likely you want to sharpen your comforting skills. Speaking for all the people I've heard from through the years: Thank you! You *can* learn to listen. You *really can help* your heartbroken friends, if you will do just one thing, truly. Love them.

Love, Without Wax

Perhaps you've heard 1 Corinthians 13 called the "Love Chapter" of the Bible. But did you realize that the apostle Paul penned those beautiful words to a group of believers who had been so marvelously blessed with divine gifts that they sometimes forgot to express them in love?

"The most excellent way" of love calls believers beyond spectacular manifestations of the Spirit – prophecy, knowledge, and supernatural faith – beyond extreme generosity and even martyrdom, to a redemptive personal involvement with each other. For love is patient, kind, not envious, boastful or proud. It isn't rude or self-seeking, isn't easily provoked nor does it keep a record of wrongs. It rejoices with truth, protects, trusts, hopes and always perseveres. And when it has these characteristics, love never fails.

Although this book is not intended as an indictment of anyone, the sad fact is that (except in rare churches) the ability to love in this way has been lost in the fast-paced, superficial experience we call "faith." It would be misleading, therefore, to let you pass this page without making it clear that *really loving your heartbroken friend may put your faith to the ultimate test.*

In New Testament days, dishonest pottery dealers would try to salvage damaged pieces of their finest and thinnest wares by rubbing wax into the cracks and then setting those pieces in the shadows in hopes a gullible buyer would purchase them. Discerning shoppers would take these items out into the light and hold them up to the sun, which easily displayed even a hairline fracture. Pottery that passed the test was "sun-tested," because it was "without wax." The word *sincere* comes from these two root words.

The only really helpful thing you have to offer a heartbroken friend is love. This book is about more than insights into the grieving process and strategies to help. At its most fundamental level, it is about finding ways to love your friends from their brokenhearted fragmentation – regardless of its cause –

toward a new sense of wholeness, through linking you and them, by faith, to the healing love of God.

It's one thing to say you love somebody. But it's an entirely different matter when, having heard your words, your hurting friend holds you up to the sun—metaphorically, of course—to see if the love you offer is really as sincere as it appears to be.

In the following chapters, you'll find many practical suggestions about how to demonstrate the reality of your love. My hope is that you'll discover how the many facets of love can match and meet the highly individualized needs of your heartbroken friends. For the fact is—you can make a real difference.

For Reflection or Discussion

1. If you are studying this in a group setting, ask each person to share what they hope to gain from the course, and why.

2. In a group setting, ask two volunteers to role-play a brief conversation between Marty (the unemployed man in the first story) and a Christian friend. When complete, choose the two or three best points each party made. Ask "Marty" what things helped and what didn't, and note these in your "practical list of dos and don'ts"—a continuing chalkboard exercise through the entire study. Print out a list for each group member at the end.

3. Identify and/or discuss what it means to *individualize your caring.*

4. Do you think the estimate that 30 percent of those in church on a Sunday morning are struggling with a broken heart too high, too low, about right? Can you offer any evidence to back up your own estimate, or is it mostly intuitive?

5. In your own experience, is the hypothetical sermon in the text typical, atypical, or highly unlikely in today's church? If you've ever heard a sermon like this, what was your reaction at the time? If positive, or at least neutral, did you wonder how some members of the congregation might be taking it?

6. While Nancy's case is rare, stories like hers are surfacing much too often these days. How could you try to meet Nancy's need of friendship without putting her privacy in this extremely delicate matter at risk?

7. What is your response to the question of what to say when you don't know what to say?
___ All things work together for good.
___ Into each life some rain must fall.
___ I'm sorry.
___ I don't know what to say, but I do love you.

___ Nothing at all.

___ Is this a trick question?

8. How could Katherine have been more helpful to Martha? After discussing this, have two volunteers role-play this conversation with more sensitivity, if you have time.

9. In 1 Corinthians 8:1, the apostle Paul says, "Knowledge puffs up, but love builds up." Yet when we try to help heartbroken people, we often give them knowledge: facts, ideas, concepts, principles. Why?

___ Truth is the only way beyond the pain.

___ Their minds have to control their emotions through knowledge.

___ It keeps them at arm's length and I don't really want to invest the energy and time to get involved.

___ If they don't take good advice, it's their problem.

___ I couldn't mail myself, so I sent a card instead.

10. In a group setting, have someone read 1 Corinthians 13:4-8a with the goal of identifying which aspects of love described there fit each illustration in this chapter.

11. Complete this statement: In order to really help my heartbroken friend, I need to:

In a group setting, share your answers, and pray that in the coming weeks you will become even more effective comforters than you are now. You will. God will honor your desire because it is aligned with God's.

2

A loneliness that must be shared

*Be the rare source
of real comfort*

SOMETIMES IT'S NEARLY impossible for heartbroken people to believe that there really is a way beyond their pain. But you can break through and give that hope, if you'll be as sensitive and creative as Alicia is in the following hypothetical dialogue with Susan, a woman recently widowed. (Note: The situation is similar to that in the previous chapter for purposes of comparison, with the exception that in this case, Alicia is also a widow.)

A: Susan, I've been thinking about you a lot and wondering how you're doing. Would this be a good time to visit for a little while?

S: Oh, come on in, Alicia. I won't be much company, but I'm glad to see you.

A: You don't have to be company, I just want to be with you.

S: Thank you.

A: How are you doing, really?

S: It depends on whom I talk to. When I'm at church and

someone asks how I am without stopping, I just say "fine." But I'm really not doing very well. Alicia, what can I do?

A: I don't know. I wish I had all the answers. But I do know there are a lot of people who care about you and a lot of people who want to be here for you. And I know you'll make it through, even if I can't tell you how. When I was widowed, I made it through, though at the time I couldn't imagine that. Sometimes I would just sit in the dark by myself for hours, staring at the clock.

S: (Nods) Me, too. But then I have to get up and get going because the kids need me. Jeremy's only ten. Heather's eight. That's the only thing that keeps me sane. Sometimes I think I'd go over the edge if I didn't have them. What am I going to do?

A: It sounds like you're doing the best you can, taking it one step at a time. For me, I also knew the kids needed me, and I would talk to myself all day, saying things like "You have to get up. You have to do something." But a lot of times I couldn't. It felt like something big was pressing me down into that chair, like I couldn't move. The clothes didn't get washed; the house didn't get cleaned ... for a long time.

S: I can relate to that, too. Sometimes, it's like I'm living in a slow motion ream. What did you do to get past it?"

A: Well, time didn't fix it, I'll tell you that. Over time, things just deteriorated. So I finally went to my doctor, and she prescribed some medications, which I didn't want to have to take, because I had this idea that Christians are supposed to be strong, and just rely on faith, and so forth. But I knew I needed something or I was going to go under, so I followed her advice. And after about a few weeks, I started feeling better. About a year after starting the meds, I didn't need them anymore.

S: People think I am strong, but I'm really not, except maybe in public. Sometimes I am so afraid and worried that I can't stop my mind from going 'round and 'round in circles—it keeps me awake at night. I can't concentrate, so I'm afraid to drive unless I absolutely must. And I've lost my appetite. I've thought of going to see a doctor, too, but I'm even afraid of that.

A: I'll go with you, if that would help. I'll drive you there, in fact.

S: You would? That would make it all a lot easier.

Loneliness is one of grief's most devastating outcomes. And depression like Susan and Alicia describe is common after losses of this magnitude, even for believers. (For more practical help on this topic, see *New Light on Depression.*)

If you really want to help your heartbroken friend in a situation like this, you'll have to find a way to intercept her retreat to the only apparently safe place left – inside herself. You'll have to find a way to convince her: Your problem is *our* problem. When you're weak, I'll help you stand. If you're afraid, I'll be with you. If you fall, I'll help you up again. And if you want to seek support (from a professional or a support group, for instance) I am willing to go with you.

Unfortunately, comforting of this ilk is a rare commodity, especially among Christians. For some reason, the church is the only army that shoots its wounded.

Purple Heartless Club

Frank and Rose Williams were both high-profile leaders in their assembly, anxious to hear the group's shared wisdom when Rose found her "dream house" and wondered if buying it would be God's will. A combination of circumstances, including finding a buyer for their current house, seemed to indicate they should.

After a great deal of prayer and encouragement by their friends, they took the plunge. But after Rose and Frank moved into the new house, their buyer backed out, and suddenly they had a serious financial crisis instead of proof positive that God was involved.

"The 'friends' who confirmed God's will to us when everything was going well now will have nothing to do with us," Rose wrote. "Our church has provided almost no support. My family doesn't understand. And I have been shaken to the core. I have gone all the way back to the beginning in my relationship with God. What does God really promise us?

"This has been the most painful experience of my life."

In some churches, where "faith" means agreeing with the current pastor's interpretation of Scripture, people are not often prepared to get dirty when disaster strikes another member. The sermons over the past year have focused on principles of positive faith, every service ending with a gospel presentation and an altar call for salvation, rededication, or in some groups, an invitation to receive the "baptism of the Spirit."

The problem is not so much with any of these components – but limiting what we call "church" to activities held in a certain building during certain time periods of the week, following a certain format led by certain trained professionals.

In New Testament times, Christians shared all things in common, including their joys and sorrows. The Greek word for this shared life is *koinonia*, from the root *koinos* which means "common." An almost identical word, *koinonos*, means "partaker" or "partner." Beyond the transforming message of new life through faith in Jesus, the most revolutionary thing those early believers offered was: One with God means one with us. From now on, we're in this *together*.

These Greek words are sometimes translated "fellowship," which in many churches today is *something you do* in a place called the "fellowship hall," where it is highly unlikely a heartbroken person is going to rain on everybody else's parade by telling the truth about how much life hurts. Perhaps it is in the nature of institutions that protocol, programs and progress gain higher priority than participating in someone else's pain.

But I have to believe the latter can happen without threatening the former in any way. In fact, *the more people become partners in life, the more they will want to become partners in faith.* But if conformity to some autocratic leader's way of seeing or doing things is all they share, both their faith and their ability to help their heartbroken friends will be deficient, and their "comforting" will degenerate into a rather sanctimonious form of abuse.

"Our church pastor made things *worse*," Rose said. "He accused us of not giving enough and of having unconfessed sin in our lives. After 14 months, we couldn't take it anymore. We found a small church where, ironically, many others have come after being hurt at other churches. Having to leave a church that was our home for nine years, and knowing that most people didn't understand why we had to go, is the thing that still hurts the most, even after two-and-a-half years."

Making a Diagnosis

I'm not indicting this person, since I've failed enough parishioners myself. For example, Sandra's battle with multiple sclerosis began when I was her pastor. Here's how she remembers my response: "[You] had serious personal problems and said 'You will have to find someone else to talk to. I can't be your pastor.'"

"There was no one else," she continued. "There never has been."

Naturally, I don't recall saying those words, but I do remember being absorbed by my own grief after Jonathan's death (see *Jonathan, You Left Too Soon*). And I do recall not knowing how to help Sandra. At least I didn't condemn her, except to the intense loneliness she described.

So instead of blaming anybody, let's view this as a diagnosis: We could be much better at bearing one another's burdens, thus fulfilling the law of Christ – the law of love. Yet, sometimes we can't even seem to fulfill the "Golden Rule."

Why should a pastor's wife, just returned from burying her beloved 28-year-old daughter – killed by a drunken driver – have to endure this statement her very first Sunday after the funeral? "I told her not to ride that motorcycle or she'd be killed."

Why should her husband have to suffer this question from another of their parishioners: "Did you go to that young man in jail and put your arm around him and tell him you loved him and forgave him?"

When the pastor said, "No, I didn't," the person added insult to injury by responding, "Well, I'll pray for you until you do."

How can it happen so consistently that we who claim to know, worship, and emulate the One who fulfilled the prophecy, "A bruised reed he will not break, and a smoldering wick he will not snuff out" (Mt 12:20) can be so insensitive toward the pain of people we're supposed to care about? After giving this a lot of thought, I think it really comes down to faulty spiritual wiring.

This same pastor now looks back in amazement at the teaching he endorsed before his daughter's death. "I used to hear a lot of preachers and other people say 'Once you become a Christian, you won't have any more problems.' I always preached that when those valleys and hard times come, God will come in a great way and you'll just be on top of the world and walk right on through with a smile on your face.

"Then we learned that good people do suffer and go through the dark night of the soul, wondering if God is there and hears them."

Identifying the Causes

One reason Job's story is so timeless is because the issues he grappled with are still common to brokenhearted people today. I'm not speaking only of the spiritual agony of feeling abandoned by God, but the emotional, physical and relational pain that came from losing first his wealth, his children and then his health, followed by his human support system, beginning with his wife who suggested he might as well curse God and die.

Job's pain intensified, however, when his three friends—Eliphaz, Bildad, and Zophar—began to attack him for trying to express a heartbreak that nearly defied words:

> Why did I not perish at birth ... ?
> For now I would be lying down in peace; ....
> Why is light given to those in misery, and life to the bitter of soul, to those who long for death that does not come, who search for it more than for hidden treasure, who are filled with gladness and rejoice when they reach the grave?
> Why is life given to a man whose way is hidden, whom God has hedged in? (Job 3:11, 13, 20-22).

Eliphaz summarizes the earliest version of what continues to be the self-righteous approach to the brokenhearted:

> But who can keep from speaking?
> Think how you have instructed many, how you have strengthened feeble hands ... [and] faltering knees.
> But now trouble comes to you, and you are discouraged; it strikes you, and you are dismayed.
> Should not your piety be your confidence and your blameless ways your hope?
> Consider now: Who, being innocent, has ever perished?
> Where were the upright ever destroyed?
> As I have observed, those who plow evil and those who sow trouble reap it....
> Blessed is the man whom God corrects; so do not despise the discipline of the Almighty.
> For he wounds, but he also binds up; he injures, but his hands also heal....
> We have examined this, and it is true.
> So hear it and apply it to yourself (Job 4:2-8, 5:17-18, 27).

Job, now one of the loneliest men who ever lived, replies:

> A despairing man should have the devotion of his friends, even though he forsakes the fear of the Almighty.
> But my brothers are as undependable as intermittent streams;...
> Now you too have proved to be of no help; you see something dreadful and are afraid....
> Do you mean to correct what I say, and treat the words of a

despairing man as wind?
You would even cast lots for the fatherless and barter away your
friend (Job 6:14-15, 21, 26-27).

Back and forth they went, Job's "comforters" condemning
him while their former mentor and role model maintained his
integrity, justifying himself and occasionally challenging God.

Job's affliction had created the same problem for both Job
and his friends. Their belief system, which he had probably
taught them—good things happen to good people and bad
things happen to bad people—might not be trustworthy.

What so "terrified" Job's comforters was this train of
thought: Job has tried with all his heart and soul to walk up-
rightly before God. If such calamity has come upon *him*, what's
to keep something even worse from happening to *us*?

Unwilling to let their categories expand to embrace both
Job's realities and God's character—too much paradox and am-
biguity for such rigid folks!—they chose the only option left:
They rejected the very person they had come to comfort.

Needed—Listeners

When you commit yourself to helping heartbroken friends,
be aware that the further you get inside their loss, the more
uncomfortable you may feel, and not just because of the intensity of *their* feelings. Your discomfort comes because what has
happened to them does not mesh very well with your understanding of who God is and how he works in our world.

But take the risk, please, not only for the sake of your
friends, who desperately need someone to share their loneliness.
You will benefit, too, by sharing the journey, because it will
expand your own circle of love while it stretches your faith.

Your main concern, especially if this helping role is new to
you, should be learning to listen. **Listen, listen, listen.** There's
no better way to pierce the loneliness of heartbreak.

Interestingly enough, this rare ability is not primarily a
passive exercise in which you function as a human tape record-

How to Help a Heartbroken Friend

er. Therapeutic listening involves learning *how to ask the right questions*, including responses intended to clarify and encourage your friend to keep going deeper. In this process, they may discover – to their surprise – *what they really think or feel* about whatever issue you're helping them process at the time. For when you're stuck in grief (or the depression related to it) there are times when you need someone else to help you put your thoughts or feelings into words.

For example, when she was really hurting, Crystal needed someone to coax her feelings out because no one had ever modeled for her how to express what was inside. "I needed someone to listen to what I was *thinking*," she said, "somebody to read my mind. In my family, you didn't talk about anything. My mother had a breakdown when I was in junior high and to this day, I don't know what caused it. All I remember is she cried every day and I couldn't help her, couldn't get to her. "So, you didn't talk about those things. I needed somebody to pull it out of me. I didn't need somebody to say, 'I'm going to listen to your heartache,' because I wouldn't know where to start."

Obviously, people differ in their ability to verbalize their hurts, so you'll need wisdom to be able to discern how to individualize your listening style to match their need. But here are some guiding principles that will fit many situations:

- Make sure you are there, with them, and not somewhere else, even if you've heard this story ten times before. One impatient glance at your watch or a vacant stare when you've just been asked a question and you'll have to work very hard to recover their trust.
- One way to stay there is to maintain eye contact and a posture that indicates you really want to hear what's being said. Lean toward the speaker and touch when appropriate.
- Give feedback instead of advice. Ask leading questions instead of making statements. For instance, you might follow an angry outburst with, "You sound upset...." But if you say, "If you don't deal with that bitterness this minute, you

can't expect God to heal you," you may get compliance without heart, which isn't real and therefore isn't worth pursuing.

- Don't react judgmentally no matter what your friend says. This may be a test to see whether you're more committed to loving your friend than defending God's reputation.
- Never say, "I know exactly how you feel," followed by a long discourse on your own heartbreaks. Your own hurts may have equipped you to understand and at some point may be useful to let the other person know you've traveled a similar path, but always keep in mind that your highest priority is *the healthy completion of your friend's journey.*
- Finally, remember, no matter how much you may wish you could help your friends recover, their problems are their problems, regardless of how far they let you inside their loneliness. In the end, they alone can choose to pursue whatever decisions or directions seem best.

In this helping relationship, you can become redemptively involved in answering Rose's question about what God really promises. If there is any single theme resounding through both Old and New Testaments in relation to heartbreak it is this: "Do not fear, for I am with you."

But it can be nearly impossible for a heartbroken person to believe this until someone like you comes alongside to, as one of my friends says, "make God visible."

For Reflection or Discussion

1. If a lot of heartbroken people sit in their family rooms staring at the clock for twelve hours at a time, as Alicia did, how can we help them?

2. If you became convinced that one of your friends was suffering from depression, what might you do to try to help?

3. Draw a picture of loneliness, and then in a group setting, have group members (as many as wish to) show their sketches. What are the common themes? Try to create a composite group sketch of what loneliness looks like.

4. In your experience (personally or by observation), is the church an army that shoots its wounded? Give examples if you agree with this sentiment. Also, brainstorm some solutions to this problem, if you think the problem exists.

5. Have you ever gone ahead with something, believing it was God's will, only to run into multiple problems, as Rose and Frank did? Share these experiences briefly, the personal and theological questions raised, and finally how a caring friend might have helped when the crisis was at its worst.

6. Rose admitted she was shaken to the core, and that she went all the way back to the beginning in her relationship with God. Why do you think she reacted so strongly?
__ She was just a big baby; after all, she owned two houses when some people never get to own even one.
__ She had bought into a false system, including its idea of who God is and how he works in the world.
__ She felt abandoned by everyone she thought cared for her.
__ She wasn't well enough versed in positive thinking.
__ Other:

7. What's more important in your own church: protocol, programs, progress, or people's problems? Prioritize the list as you think God sees things.

8. Do you think it's true the more people become partners in life, the more they will want to become partners in faith?
__ Sounds a little New-Agey to me.
__ Puts the cart before the horse. Faith is first, life second.
__ I don't understand what "partners in life" means.
__ It's about time we stopped separating these.

9. Could you understand why Rose said "Having to leave a church that was our home for nine years ... hurts the most"? In a group setting, try to decide which of the following hurts the most and why: ostracized by friends, condemned by friends, misunderstood by friends, ignored by friends.

10. If you were the pastor whose daughter had been killed by the drunk driver, how would you have reacted to the parishioner's question: "Did you go to that young man in jail and put your arm around him and tell him you loved him and forgave him?" Why might people feel obligated to say such things?

11. In a group setting, have two volunteers role-play the first interchange of Job and Eliphaz in a modern context based on Job 3:1-7:21. Why do you think Job's friends reacted as they did? Are any of their reactions still common today?

12. Job complained that his "brothers were as undependable as intermittent streams." Is there a modern way to express this dilemma that compounds the pain of our travel companions?

13. Do good things happen to good people and bad things happen to bad people?

14. Create your own list of emotions, with a view toward helping your heartbroken friend accurately label how she feels.

15. Once you've created this list, role-play a conversation between Crystal and her friend.

16. Share any insights you may have in terms of how to reassure your friend, through your involvement, that God's promise to be with her is true.

Pray that the Lord will show you creative ways to communicate this truth to heartbroken people in your church. God will.

3

An emptiness that must be filled

Fill it with yourself.

CHRISTINE WAS ABUSED beyond what most of us can imagine. "I lost my childhood," she wrote. "At the age of 28 I began remembering things that confirmed that as a child I was physically and sexually abused in very violent ways by my parents and the satanic cult they were involved in. When I got into therapy, I discovered that all the blank spots throughout my childhood were my way of wiping away the ugly stuff."

A lot of people draw a blank when they remember their childhood. Sometimes it's only with the help of a skilled counselor that they are able to fill in what happened and realize that the unconscious source of what's been driving them for as long as they can recall is an *intense inner search to fill a void* they can't even define. But they do know this: *Something's missing.*

Of course, it's nearly impossible for disinterested observers to offer much real help to someone like Christine, although that doesn't necessarily keep them from offering advice. "People didn't understand the depth of my pain," she said, "but they still offered advice like, 'You just need to have a better self-image.' Yeah, right, like I can bake it up in the oven and suddenly, poof, out comes a wonderful self-image. Give me a break, please. I'd like to see others go through what I have and come out with a rosy self-image."

She Had Everything, but Was Empty Inside

Even affluence can create a vacuum like this. Misty grew up in a very materialistic, upper-middle-class family, surrounded by everything she ever wanted or needed, from clothes to cars, except one thing: nurturing love.

In her case, emotional deprivation was the norm, combined with a lot of pressure to look good and perform well. Once when she was six, she was left behind at a fashion show where *she had been the emcee*. Later that night her mother gave birth to her sister.

Her father, a salesman, was never home. Her mother, although there physically, was very unstable. The only communication she recalls was "Clean your room."

When Misty was 19 her parents divorced, which further devastated the little girl inside the now-grown-woman's body who still longed for some kind of relationship with her parents.

When everything seemed to be falling apart Misty held together because she had become a Christian and was attending a Christian college in her hometown. Also, without realizing why, she had begun latching on to older women in a desperate effort to find the mother's love she'd never known.

This went on until Misty was 24, still searching for somebody to tuck her into bed at night. Finally, she found Stacy, a woman with a family of her own who was willing to love Misty unconditionally and commit to being her friend, whatever it took, until Misty's emotional wounds were healed.

Stacy, acting on the advice of Misty's counselor, tried to create for the younger woman the childhood things she'd missed. She tucked Misty into bed with words the young woman had never heard, "Good night, love."

Such tender moments had their down side, however, because Misty grew to hate herself for needing them. "I started causing problems in the relationship because it was good," Misty recalls. "I didn't know how to deal with *good*. I could deal with turmoil, so if there wasn't turmoil, I created it."

In other words, regardless of how desperate Misty was to fill an inner vacuum that she described as a bottomless pit, in one part of herself she needed the emptiness because it was the only thing she had ever known. This is the reason children of alcoholics marry alcoholics, or victims of various abuses keep going back to their abusers. It may feel bad to feel bad, but at least there's some familiar security in it.

Stacy and Misty have been through a lot together in the past seven years, but one of the most helpful things Stacy did for her younger friend was to teach her how to nurture and sustain herself.

For instance, nobody had ever rocked Misty, so Stacy gave her a rocking chair, and taught her to rock herself, to visualize Stacy rocking her, or her own mother rocking her. Now Misty's house is full of rocking chairs.

"She also helped me visualize a healing place, the place where I wanted to go," Misty said, "because I got so frustrated with how long my healing was taking. *She* could see the changes, but the increments were so small *I* couldn't see them myself. In order to illustrate where I was headed, she read me that childhood story about the moonflower that blossoms at night. She told me I would know when I was healed, and she would know it, too. And she promised to give me that story as a milestone when the day finally came. Shortly after I moved to Colorado, a package arrived from Stacy. It was the moonflower story, written out in longhand."

Creative Nurturing

Not everyone has an internal void as significant as Misty's or Christine's, yet their journeys illustrate how competent adults (they both served with Christian ministries) can conceal a need that only good friends can meet.

Counselors are helpful, yes, especially in the initial stages of discovering where the holes are. But the long-term healing for emptiness like this takes a far deeper involvement in a person's life than any counselor is able to fulfill. Misty's story is about how an untrained woman who cared became the front-line helper while the counselors became the support team as time went on.

We live in such a specialized society that when someone like Misty comes into our lives, instead of trying to help them, we refer them as quickly as possible to some professional. But, as one of my psychiatrist friends reminded me, before there were psychiatrists, there were friends.

You can help the Mistys that you already know – you might be surprised how many there are – but to do it you'll have to be willing to pay the kind of price their inner healing will require of you.

You see, they can't fill the hole themselves. Somebody has to fill it for them, then *with* them, and then *show* them how to fill it themselves. Ideas won't do it. Principles, techniques and advice may help, but only a *person* can fill the kind of hole we're talking about, because only a person has the flexibility to discern the uniqueness of each individual's inner need and then create a personalized, healing balm to match it.

Occasionally, as Stacy discovered, the one who is trying to help must *personally* take the place of what is missing, at least until the brokenhearted friend has received what was lost (or never offered). When this happens, you will be fulfilling a role like that of the Old Testament "scapegoat" upon whose head was placed the sins of the people on the Day of Atonement, and who was driven into the wilderness afterward.

This symbolized Jesus' role on the cross, when he volun-

How to Help a Heartbroken Friend

tarily took upon himself the sins of all who would believe in him, and then entered the wilderness of abandonment when he said, "My God, my God, why have you forsaken me?" (Mk 15:34). When you choose to take upon yourself the heartbreak of another to this degree, you are becoming as much like Christ as you will ever be. But don't be surprised how much it hurts. Caring costs. There's no way around it. Yet, in the end, the joy of seeing your heartbroken friend healed will far outweigh any of your expenses in the process. Stacy would certainly agree with that.

Laughing on the Outside, but ...

Unfortunately, sometimes children are forced into a scapegoat role by their parents. When this happens another kind of internal vacancy occurs.

Jeremy's father was a livestock wrangler in Hollywood. If there was a stampede, he was the one who created it, then rounded up the cattle while the cameras were still rolling. His mother, on the other hand, seemed "to live in a constant state of emotional trauma," Jeremy said. "To this day, trouble just seems to seek her out. She lives a turbulent life; there's never any peace."

Jeremy still battles with some of the issues bequeathed to him by his parents. His mother, apparently working with his dad, had a horse fall on her, crushing one of her legs. By the time bad had turned to worse, her body was reacting to the steel pin in her leg, and she ended up a drug addict through the opium-derivative medication she received for her pain.

"Sometime in this whole scenario," he said, "my mom and dad got into a real bad argument, and Mom went out to a bar where she got drunk. The bartender took advantage of her, raped her and made her pregnant. She tried to abort this baby by riding roller-coasters and horses and giving her body a generally hard time, but nothing worked. In the middle of it all, my father left us."

After the baby was born and given to another family to raise, Jeremy's father returned, but now he was abusive, beating his wife and children with whips. The sad result was that this little boy became his mother's main support system.

"We didn't have anything," Jeremy recalls. "We moved to the backwoods of Texas into a little house with two rooms and no furniture, except a table that was made out of a door and a couple of sawhorses. Strange as it sounds, though, I had a horse. I remember riding that horse when I was really little, playing Lone Ranger. But then one December my mother asked me if I was willing to sell my horse so we could have a Christmas."

Little Jeremy's problem was that his parents were so busy fighting, there was never anybody there for him. No one to talk to or share with. No one to fill the emptiness inside.

So to fill a void that must be filled, Jeremy turned to sex, primarily because when he was a boy one of his male cousins had been sexually abusive toward him, lighting a fire of lust that turned into an addiction before he became an adult.

"I was always looking for someone to be there for me," he said, "but I didn't even know what that meant. I didn't understand. You walk out into the cruel world and you say, 'Whoa! Where am I? Now what do I do?'"

Jeremy enlisted in the military because he figured it would teach him discipline, but all he learned in the Air Force was how to circumvent the system. The only good result was that his assignment brought him to Las Vegas where he met his future wife Toni, then a patient in a psychiatric hospital, when he went to visit *her roommate*.

Here was an opportunity to fulfill the only role in which Jeremy was comfortable—saving the failing female. The net result, predictably, had its ups and downs.

Even though Jeremy was internalizing stress he didn't deserve and trying to fill a hole he didn't understand, on the outside he was "a funny guy, a barrel of laughs to be around. But nobody knew who I was. *I didn't know who I was*." Jeremy, the funny guy, was a living example of Proverbs 14:13, "Even in laughter the heart may ache, and joy may end in grief."

One of his most poignant comments was, "It was only after I became a Christian that I wanted to kill myself, put a gun to my head; because then I began to see the truth and I couldn't handle it. I could pretend, block it out, fake it, but I couldn't handle the truth when I started learning a lot of things about myself."

The Helper's Dilemma

Here's the problem, in bold print: **Starting to learn things about yourself begins with finding a friend willing to help you separate truth from fantasy. But sorting out the truth can be excruciatingly painful for people like Christine or Misty or Jeremy, because maintaining the fantasy feels so much better.**

Beyond the resistance – even antagonism – that may arise when you try to help somebody like this, working with them can tap unconscious fears in yourself, because most of us have some kind of hole we're desperately trying to fill.

Here are some suggestions if you decide to embrace the extreme needs heartbroken people like these may present:

- Take every suicidal comment seriously. Don't pretend you didn't hear. Instead, say something like this: "I can understand how you might want to escape from all of this, but I care very much about you and I want you to live. So if you insist on talking like this, I'll have no other choice but to take you seriously and call someone to protect you from yourself. Now tell me, how serious are you?"
- Don't fill your friend's void with nothing, specifically, words, concepts (including theological concepts) or platitudes. Their need is far more complicated than that. Only a *person* can meet it, starting with you, but ultimately leading to another, even more able Person who understands what it means to feel abandoned.

- Realize that the reason you want to withdraw (if you do) is because the need your friend is expressing is either way beyond what you think you can handle or in an area that you would rather leave undisturbed in your own psyche. Face the truth squarely – and move on.
- Be patient. Blamers who have been scapegoats need to tell their story over and over and over again. Look for an opportunity to short-circuit the cycle, once you have proven your loyalty, by saying: "I've heard you describe this before. Can we stop for just a moment and talk about it?"
- Be ready to become a scapegoat yourself, specifically, to take the emotional pain upon your own head, so this person can move beyond bondage to it. While this is happening, be sure you have your own partner to support you in prayer.
- But, even with your prayer partner, never divulge the other person's secrets. People with "holes" often dump a lot of garbage. But if you reveal confidences and this becomes known to the person you are trying to help, you may *never be able to recover that same level of trust.*
- Try to discover not only what the person's inner vacuum is, and how it happened, but also how to creatively fill it.

Here is the way Stacy tried to do this for Misty, once she realized what Misty's needs really were. Stacy gave her younger friend "Misty's Love Alphabet," written out, one letter at a time, on the pages of a sticky pad:

A: Misty is authentic. (Not phoney)
B: Misty is beautiful. (Not only physically)
C: Misty is comforting. (Reaches out to people who are hurting)
D: Misty is deep. (She looks for more than superficial characteristics)
E: Misty is energetic. (Loads a dishwasher fast)
F: Misty is fervent. (Intensely devoted)

G: Misty is generous. (Gives out of love)

H: Misty is home-loving. (Loves the qualities of home)

I: Misty is insightful. (Sees with more than eyes)

J: Misty is just. (Sees fairness in all things)

K: Misty is kind. (Not mean)

L: Misty is lovable. (Easy to love)

M: Misty is a mother's delight. (I'm proud of her)

N: Misty is needed. (She's important to me)

O: Misty is outstanding. (No ordinary girl here!)

P: Misty is poised. (She handles different situations with aplomb)

Q: Misty is quality. (Knows good stuff and is good stuff)

R: Misty is responsible. (Always dependable)

S: Misty is spunky. (Spirited, plucky)

T: Misty is trustworthy. (She can be trusted to do it, keep it, say it)

U: Misty is understanding. (Perceptive, fine tuned)

V: Misty is valued highly. (By many, mainly Stacy)

W: Misty is wonderful. (Amazing, remarkable, very fine)

X: Misty is X-tra. (Out of the ordinary)

Y: Misty says yes. (She is open to receive love from many)

Z: Misty has zest. (Keen pleasure in living and loving)

Through Spirit-driven creativity like this, even something as common as a sticky-pad can become a life-transforming epistle to fill a love-starved soul. If you know someone who struggles to fill an emptiness he or she has entrusted to you, ask the Lord to show you a way to start.

For Reflection or Discussion

1. When Christine began to fill in what was missing in her childhood – through the help of a qualified counselor – she discovered some truly sinister memories. It is possible that by reading her story, you have been reminded of something similar? If so, how do you plan to process this pain? What help

could a friend be in this journey? Do you have the professional support you need?

2. Do you agree that emotional deprivation creates the same kind of inner vacuum as ritual sexual abuse? Defend your position.

3. Have you ever had a friend like Stacy? Describe how that person helped fill some void in your life.

4. Recall the way your mother (or father) tucked you into bed with words like, "Good night, love." How is this reflected in the way you perceive God's love for you today?

5. Discuss the implications of this statement: "Before there were psychiatrists, there were friends."

6. Have you ever witnessed anybody playing the "I'm-your-father, I'm-your-mother game"? Describe the dynamics without violating anybody's privacy. In a group setting, if several members of your group feel strongly enough about this, have volunteers create a role-play on this theme.

7. Have you ever personally been somebody's scapegoat, either by their choice or yours? Describe the feelings involved. Is there some redemptive use for this role today? If so, how can a person embrace it for the good of another?

8. Have you known anyone who was laughing on the outside but crying on the inside? If you got through the façade, what did you discover that person's real issue was?

9. Identify some common "platitudes" that amount to "filling your friend's void with nothing."

10. Start to create a love alphabet for Jeremy, based on what you know about his story. If there is someone you are working with now who has an emptiness such as this chapter discusses, find a simple way to give a gift such as this, and watch what happens.

4

Healing the wounds
on their own terms

*They won't heal any other
way*

FOR 15 YEARS Buffy was Gary's best friend. Gary's parents and
grandparents had all died by the time he was 21, and he had no
brothers or sisters. Gary never married either, so Buffy, his
horse, filled a huge need in the middle-aged fellow's life.

Suddenly, however, Buffy got very sick and had to be put
to sleep. As a result, Gary had what he called a "mental breakdown" because he had loved his horse so deeply. The hurt was
so great, Gary didn't have the heart to love any other person
or animal. He wasn't suicidal or bitter; just tired. He felt totally
useless and was convinced there was no point in his staying
alive. Every day, he prayed that God would let him die. When
this failed, he wondered if he was being punished. Convinced
that he would never know lasting peace or happiness in this
world, he wanted to go to a place where these things would
become reality.

Gary's psychologist speculated that he was experiencing

delayed grieving in relation to all the losses in his life. Gary tried to agree, but for him the real grief was being left behind. He simply wanted to be where his family and pets were.

The clergy he consulted scoffed at the idea that his pets were in heaven, but he couldn't imagine heaven without them. After all, he figured, God made animals before humans, and Jesus talked about the value to God of even a little sparrow.

Evidently, Gary's heartbreak was an anomaly to his would-be comforters. The psychologist wanted to theorize it away and the ministers wanted to theologize it away, but Gary's problem remained – How do I find a way to embrace living when all my friends have died?

By phone and by letter, I tried to address both sides of this heartbroken person's need. Theologically (or intellectually) I told him I thought there was more evidence than not in the Bible that when God has made the new heavens and the new earth, people and animals will be there and be friends again. But, I added, I also expect that the glory of God and the wonder of being with God will so far outweigh the other joys (or reunion with those who have gone before, whether human or not) that they will seem pale by comparison. The problem, we will then know (as C.S. Lewis wrote), is not that we loved the others too much, but that we loved God not enough.

Gary's real problem was that his heart had been broken – again – and he was afraid to allow himself to love anyone, or anything – again. Behind all that was a heart full of love, so as I recall, I suggested that he get involved with an animal shelter where there would be many animals with an unlimited need for what he had to give. I should have suggested, also, that he seek help from a medical professional experienced in treating depression since Gary's perspective was no doubt clouded by the gray lenses through which this disorder causes people to view the world. (For a comprehensive treatment of this subject, see *New Light on Depression*.)

Gary's professional comforters had tried (rather unsuccess-

How to Help a Heartbroken Friend

fully, as far as I could see) to help him beyond his heartbreak by forcing his reaction through their framework (psychological and religious) instead of authenticating his reaction by engaging his heartbreak on its own terms (and turf). Gary needed to hear, both verbally and non-verbally, "It's only normal to mourn the loss of a close friend – and Buffy was the best friend you had. Your hurt is a testimony to that."

Answering Questions Nobody's Asking

I've been on both sides of this issue myself. I've preached funeral sermons with a "salvation" message and even an invitation *when nobody was asking "How can I be saved?"* I've sat through two funeral sermons related to my son Jonathan (there were two services) that addressed a lot of issues, but not the ones that haunted me: "If this is what I get for serving God, what's the use, anyway?" or "How can I love and serve a God who either causes or allows such things to happen?"

Even in my counseling, I would listen to clients describe their situations and then tell them what *I'd been through and how I'd handled it*, when what they needed was not another load on top of theirs, but someone to say, "You've really been through a lot; would you help me understand how it feels?"

If you're really going to help your heartbroken friends, you'll have to meet them in the center of their own pain and convince them to let you walk with them through it to the other side. Informing them what their issues are – because these are the ones you're most familiar and comfortable with – and where they must head in order to resolve their hurt *may actually seem to help them in the short run*. The hurting person may say the right things and do the right things, and have every appearance of doing well when, for example, the pastor makes a post-funeral visit. But after the pastor leaves with a positive feeling about where the person is headed, only a few months later the pastor, along with everyone else in the church, is totally surprised when that same person goes over the edge, one way or another. Denial is a boomerang that always comes back to hit somebody in the face.

"Dealing with" heartbreak in *any* prepackaged way *cannot really help* over the long term (otherwise known as real life) because sooner or later heartbroken persons realize that the answers they've embraced and acted upon had nothing to do with their real questions, still unresolved.

If or when this happens, it may usher in this potentially detrimental, but logical, sequence of thought: *When my heart was broken, nobody would hear me out. Instead, they pressured me to accept answers to questions they thought I should be asking instead of the ones I really wanted to ask. But now it's clear that their best answers don't fit my real questions, so I'll just search for my answers somewhere else.*

Rushing Things Just Makes it Longer

As you may recall from the previous chapter, Jeremy met his future wife Toni when she was a patient in a psychiatric hospital. Toni had been hospitalized after one of her numerous suicide attempts – her way of trying to escape the heartbreak of her adolescence when her father sexually abused her for years until he made her pregnant at age 16.

Jeremy, already well trained by his mother as a rescuer, spent the first few years of their marriage trying to rescue Toni. "I'm a good example of what not to do," Jeremy admitted. "Most times when this poor woman was trying to share something with me, I just wanted to fix it. 'You know, you should do this' and so forth. My tendency was to say, 'Okay, now what do we do to get beyond this? Let's get out the Bondo, patch this puppy up and get on down the road.'"

"Jeremy never meant to hurt me by asking 'What are we going to do to get over this?'" Toni said. "But I was supposed to jump right into his solution and I wasn't ready for that. I really needed to bellyache for about six years."

Nobody else wanted to hear it, either. "Sympathy, to me,

has always been a thumbs-down," Toni said. "I'd tell people everything that was bothering me and they would treat me like, 'What do you want, sympathy?' or 'How many years ago did you say that was?'

"I'm in the depths of despair and I'm so weak and no one can pull me out of it. All they can say is 'Toughen up!' Well, I'm not ready to toughen up. I'll be tough when I'm good and ready."

If your heartbroken friends had a dollar for every time they heard "Don't you think you should be over it by now?" they could take you on a trip to DisneyWorld. The problem is, until they are over it, they won't care to go along themselves.

Although there is no divinely inspired timetable for various types of loss, most people seem to have one. My heartbroken friends who returned surveys related to my preparation of this book often mentioned how impatient, and unkind, people could be. Here are a few choice remarks I hope you'll never make:

- *You'll get over this and your life will be normal again.* A bereaved mother whose 23-year-old son, a deputy sheriff, had been killed on duty by a drunk driver said, "I have not recovered and never will. A part of me died with him. Well-meaning people tried to force me back into my daily routine before I had a chance to deal with this tragedy."

- *You're too depressed to be around.* "This was three months after Timothy was stillborn," a young woman wrote. "A pastor-friend believed Scripture says we should not grieve and that God is disappointed with us and our hardness of heart if we do." (Note: the Scripture he most likely had in mind was 1 Th 4:13 where Paul says that believers need not grieve the death of another believer, like [or, in the same way as] the rest of humanity grieves similar losses, since they have no hope. The apostle's point is not that believers should not grieve, but that our grieving is different, because of the hope that we have through faith in Christ.)

- *Well, I guess it's all over now.* A man said this to a woman about three weeks after the funeral of her seven-year-old. "My own mother made comments like that when at four weeks I was depressed somewhat," she adds.

- *When are you going to get rid of that wheelchair?* "As if I could make up my mind and get well," wrote a woman with multiple sclerosis. "But the classic came from an older lady: 'When you first came to our church, it seemed you would be such an asset. And now you are one of those people who is always needing something.'"

A missionary summed up the kind of patient involvement required if you really are going to meet your friend's heartbreak on its own terms. This woman struggled with a "destructive addiction," from which the only logical escape she could see was suicide: "People expressed impatience or dissatisfaction with me ... but their expectations hindered my waiting on the Lord. Many people are oblivious to their own weaknesses and avoid getting into situations that are difficult to handle. When they see others struggling, some become judgmental or critical.

"We get uncomfortable with someone else who is trying," the missionary added, "and instead of rejoicing in truth, get angry at having our own weakness exposed. Being brokenhearted involves facing one's own weaknesses, sins, limitations. For people to be empathetic, they have to be willing to become brokenhearted. Not many are willing to enter into such brokenness."

Time Alone Heals Nothing

Some people say that time heals. But some wounds are only healed by love—love over a long period of time. God made us all different—intellectually, temperamentally, spiritually, not to mention male and female; and we've all been influenced by culture (education, media, role models) and subculture (family, church, peer group) about how to handle heartbreak. Because of this, no two people, including spouses who love each other deeply, can respond identically to a shared devastating event, either in terms of how long recovering takes or what methods they use to cope with the pain.

If there is anything that surprises heartbroken couples (as well as their friends) it is this: Heartbreak is a better wedge than it is a glue. Depending on the circumstances, marriage partners may be thrown together initially by the sheer force of the event, but unless they work very hard at understanding and helping one another process the feelings unique to each, they will begin at some point to diverge in their pilgrimage with pain. If your heartbroken friend is married, this is one of the factors you will need to keep in mind if you're going to help.

"Dan and I reacted quite differently to our daughter's death, right from the beginning," Mary said. "He took the early morning call, and when I heard him say, 'Not my Minny!' I knew I didn't want to hear it. He wanted to be held, but I couldn't stand to be held. I just threw back the covers and said, 'I have to do something.'

"I don't even remember what I did, but I had to be busy. I thought that a husband and wife would be together, but it seemed from that moment like Dan went one way and I went another. He became a couch potato and I rushed around, 90 miles an hour. He wanted to take a vacation and I couldn't stand to because it would be too much time to think.

"Instead, I walked. I walked miles and miles. I cleaned the house, cleaned the car and I overdid everything, but you do anything you can, just to survive. I bounced off every wall in the place. The person I had invested my life in was gone. My faith went out the window. God just seemed a long way away."

By contrast, Dan, a pastor for 30 years, said, "Mary suffered with grief a long time. She carries it more. I've tried to analyze why we're so different and I think it goes way back to when I was nine and my mother died. The way I coped with that then is the way I still cope with grief today: If I don't think about it, the pain goes away."

"We talked about putting on our happy faces when we went to church," Mary added, "but I noticed that Dan started spending more and more hours in front of the TV, alone. He became a recluse."

"I think I withdrew because I was disappointed in the parishioners' reactions," Dan said. "I guess I hoped that when I came home from the funeral, things would be a little bit easier, that maybe they'd let up their relentless attack. But it didn't happen. So I just didn't want to be around people. I could get up, go to church, and preach, but as soon as church was over, I'd just go home, close the door, and pull the curtains."

I could identify with Dan's experience. After Jonathan died, I still had to preach, teach, evangelize, counsel and visit – all on an emotionally empty tank. I'd drag myself out of the slough of despond (which in my case was filled with the quicksand of guilt) just far enough to carry out my Sunday duties before sliding into the muck again by Monday morning. I knew some of my parishioners cared, and they tried to help. But others disapproved of my depression and were anxious for me to get back on the pastoral saddle as if nothing had happened, which added even more guilt to my already unwieldy load.

I'll never forget how I tried, in one deacons' meeting, to express my inadequacy and fears. I just couldn't force myself out the door, midweek, to do the visitation that was expected. I needed help and I was asking for it from them. But instead of figuring out how they could share this function with me (which I believed was as much their responsibility as mine), one old-timer settled the matter by saying, "The people are waiting for the pastor to visit."

I suppose some good came of all that pain when I chronicled the journey in my first book, *Jonathan, You Left Too Soon*. But analyzing myself to death and then writing a ruthlessly honest case study about that process was the ballad of one broken and very lonely man who slogged along through solitary sorrows hoping that time and a change of venue might bring him back to the light of day.

The venue changed, but the path continued. Five years after moving to a para-church ministry, my second son, Christopher, was stricken with the same rare, genetically linked, brain-damaging illness that had killed Jonathan. This time, I took the road more traveled than many would care to admit. Desperate for something, anything to take the pain away, if only for a moment, I found myself drawn toward an illicit relationship. Only by God's grace did I manage to choose another route. (The story is chronicled in *If God Is So Good, Why Do I Hurt So Bad?* Christopher, by the way, survived and is doing very well now, having graduated from college in 2002.)

How to Minister to Your Minister

Just in case the heartbroken person you're trying to help is your pastor, I have a few suggestions, all aimed at overcoming Dan's summary of his journey with heartbreak: "There was no one there for me." Pastors may seem to be way "up there" somewhere and you may feel you can't really understand, but I promise you: *You don't have to understand your pastors, as long your pastors understand that you care.*

Don't:
- Re-preach one of their sermons or quote Romans 8:28.
- Judge them – they feel bad enough already.
- Tell them they should be over this already.
- Remind them that people are watching, so they should be a good example.
- Pray *for* them (in the sense that it's *their* problem).

Do:
- Allow them to be human – they are, you know. Allow them to express their emotions and accept them when they do.
- Love them; put your arm around them.

- Take them on an outing – picnicking or golfing or whatever you used to enjoy doing together.
- Give them time, as much as they need.
- Pray *with* them (in the sense that it's *our* problem).

In doing these things, you'll be acting like Jesus, mending a bruised reed, renewing a smoldering wick so that others will be blessed when this person's ability to minister is restored.

To use another analogy, I planted an orchard in New Hampshire and enjoyed seeing how those small fruit trees began to grow. Sometimes their small trunks would become damaged, perhaps nicked by a mower. If I noticed it soon enough and bound that wounded bark back in place, the tree could heal itself. But if I waited too long and the wound became diseased or dried out, that little tree might be in danger of not surviving long enough to produce fruit.

This same kind of binding up can be applied to broken hearts, but timing is essential and care is a must. Before you go to try to accomplish being a helper, pray *for yourself*, something like this:

> Lord, help me be discerning enough to understand what is happening with my friend, wise enough to speak the right words at the right time, and sensitive enough to do so in a therapeutic way. Help me discard perceptions and expectations that arise from a purely human point of view and utilize, instead, the insight that only your Spirit can give. My friend needs help, Lord, and I believe you want me to try to provide it. But I am afraid, afraid of my inadequacy to share this hurt in a way that will take us both toward wholeness. So I entrust us both into your grace, believing you will help me help my heartbroken friend. Amen.

For Reflection or Discussion

1. In a group setting, have a volunteer with deep affection for a pet play the role of Gary, whose horse Buffy has died. Have two other members play the parts of the counselor and the pastor, respectively, each in their professional office. Following these interchanges, debrief, asking each role player to share their reaction, followed by the group's perception of what has taken place. Try, especially, to answer these questions: Was Gary's depression legitimate? How would you try to help him?

2. What happens to a helping relationship when the helper forces the other person's issues through their own framework? If this has happened to you personally, share its result.

3. Discuss the difference between "dealing with" a person's heartbreak and "entering their pain" to understand and share it.

4. In your experience, have you been the recipient of answers to questions you weren't asking? Describe this encounter to the group, and see if you can suggest another approach that might have been more helpful.

5. Review and discuss the "choice remarks I hope you'll never make." If you have made comments like these when trying to help a heartbroken friend, how might you have expressed differently what you meant to communicate?

6. Jeremy was constantly trying to fix up Toni, who needed something else from him. In a group setting, ask a couple of volunteers to role play this typical male-female difference in the following case: The female was kidnapped six months ago, held for ransom, threatened with sexual assault, but rescued before this actually took place. She still has nightmares, especially since the trial is now underway, but her husband seems more relieved that she is home safe and he would prefer to put this all behind them and get on with life.

7. How do you react when you hear that missionaries sometimes have "destructive addictions"?

__ Not surprised – they're human.

__ Worried – that my support may be funding something like that.

__ Depressed – if it happens to them, it can happen to me.

__ Disappointed – that all our heroes turn out to have clay feet.

8. What do you think would happen to a missionary's financial base if the details of a very difficult addictive struggle became public? Suppose this missionary, home on furlough, has come to stay with you and you learn the addiction was substance abuse and the missionary is worried the temptations will recur upon return to Germany. How would you try to help?

9. If your heartbroken friend says that the way they handle loss is not to think about it so the pain goes away, is it better to accept this or to force them to talk about it?

10. In Luke 7:31-35, Jesus puts an intriguing message in the mouths of marketplace children: "We played the flute for you, and you did not dance; we sang a dirge and you did not cry." Examine the larger context, then discuss the lesson here in terms of responding appropriately to different situations:

__ Market-goers can be a pretty mellow group.

__ Stereotypes don't fit when it comes to Jesus.

__ Some people can't express extreme emotions.

__ There's no "religiously correct" approach to joy or loss.

__ Followers of Jesus should feel free to fully experience life's joys and sorrows.

11. The apostle Paul put it another way: "Rejoice with those who rejoice; mourn with those who mourn" (Rm 12:15). Which of these is more difficult and why? How can we learn to share life more fully with our friends?

5

Becoming your friend's soul mate

We'll survive this—and we'll do it together

ONE OCTOBER DAY in 1989, Jenny's 21-year-old daughter Angie was talking with her boyfriend about their future. It wasn't really an argument, but in the middle of it she got up and walked into another room (with him following), picked up his handgun, swung it around, and it went off. The police recorded Angie's death as an accidental, self-inflicted gunshot wound, since there was no depression, no suicidal ideation, no clues. Nobody will ever know if it was intentional or not.

"As you know," Jenny wrote to me, "Christians can be less than kind and this is a superb gossip opportunity. If one more person says, 'Read your Bible and pray, dear,' I may become unkind myself."

At first people visited and called, sent cards and brought food. This was especially helpful, because Jenny's husband and their five other children still needed to eat. It was all Jenny could do to heat up what had been provided, but nearly impossible for her to function well enough to carry on her normal routine.

What kept Jenny sane was a professional counselor who allowed her to yell in anger at God about the unfairness of it all. The counselor also taught her enough coping skills to survive the journey, including exercise, relaxation techniques, visualization techniques, blocking, remembering that others also hurt, taking parenting one day at a time, journaling and personal two- to three-day retreats. The only coping strategy that connected her directly with another person, however, was to "call someone." In other words, if she wanted help, *she had to ask for it*, a very difficult thing for a devastated person to do until the only other option is jumping off a high bridge. Heartbreak is a lonely road.

What made it worse was Jenny's feeling that everybody, including God, had turned their back on her. "Friends and acquaintances literally walked away," Jenny wrote, "crossed the street, turned around in a store aisle, quickly walked past me, and so on.

"I expected they would be there for us and let us hurt," Jenny added. "I know they do care, but simply have no understanding of how to demonstrate that. Love is not enough; it has to be love with action. Love enough to carry a piece of my pain as they share my hurt. The church was our major social life, so our social structure fell apart. We were just plain ignored by most of our church, judged by some. I really struggle with the realization that my non-Christian friends have been much more *there* than my Christian friends. Why?"

One friend leveled with her, at least, "You guys have been through so much [a whole series of crises] and you always thanked God through it all, smiling along the way. You're crying now and we don't know what to do with you."

"Well," Jenny noted, "I don't know what to do with me either."

Her pastor didn't come over until a month after the funeral

and when he did, he said, "I have trouble dealing with death." But the real kicker occurred when a letter arrived from her own brother, a minister, saying, "I can't absolve her; you'll have to accept that she's probably in hell."

By contrast, a person with no theological ax to grind might hug Jenny, and after using some expletive to describe her trouble, say, "Fate is fate, but friends are friends. If we don't help each other, nobody else will."

Here Come da' Judge

The comments I've received from disappointed people like Jenny are frightfully consistent in terms of how their Christian friends have not only failed to help them but added to their hurt by their misguided "comfort."

I've identified four styles of "comforting" through the years, the first two of which are detrimental, the third neutral and the fourth the only one that really helps: the critic/judge; the advice-giver; the identifier; the soul mate. Let's examine each of these and its effect, because many would-be helpers have not given their helping styles enough thought, including how *the way they're trying to help may be hindering their friend's progress toward wholeness.*

For the sake of visualizing this, let's say your friend Charlie has fallen into a pit filled with slime, which is threatening to pull him under. If he works at it, even a little, he can keep his head (or at least his nose) barely out of the sludge. If he gives up, he'll slide under and drown, a temptation that increases with time because the longer he treads muck the more exhausted he becomes. Charlie cannot climb out because the sides are too steep and slippery. If he is going to survive, he needs help.

Along comes the critic/judge who, upon seeing Charlie in the pit, polishes his halo, grabs his Bible and loudly recites five reasons why people fall into pits. The more self-righteous the orator, the more personalized will be the judgment pronounced. In general, it sounds like this: "People fall into pits because they have sin in their lives, but if you will yet repent, perhaps the Lord will rescue you."

When my first son Jonathan became ill, several of the younger men in the church speculated that God let this happen because I was materialistic. After Jonathan died, I confessed to a local Christian physician that I thought I had loved my son more than anything, perhaps maybe more than I loved God. "Then maybe that's why God had to take him," he replied.

But in terms of incredibly inappropriate remarks, the one that takes the cake came after Christopher was also stricken. A certain sanctimonious person left a note with my father (also a minister) saying that God had brought all this affliction on my father's tent because he had failed to use the King James Version of the Bible exclusively in his preaching.

The problem is, when you're simply struggling to survive, and wondering *just as much as everybody else* why such a catastrophe has befallen you, you're tempted to believe nonsense like this, because anything, even a lie, seems to provide a more secure footing than the instability of not knowing.

Speaking for myself and all the "Charlies" of this world, let me say to the judges and critics who seem to multiply when tragedy strikes: *Don't play God with us.*

Megaphonic Expertise

Since Charlie's still in the pit, let's observe how advice-givers try to help. Equipped with one of those fancy new electronic megaphones (indoors, they wear wireless mikes), the advisors strut around the pit (careful not to get too close lest they get their white shoes dirty) shouting instructions.

"You should try my five principles for pit escapement, or my four foundations for worry-free living. Or how about three steps to overcoming adversity? Name it, claim it, pretend it doesn't hurt. If you will believe in your heart there is no pit, and confess with your mouth that you are standing on solid ground, your problems will disappear. There are no tragedies, after all, only opportunities for God to manifest power in your life."

When Naomi was 18 months old, spinal meningitis stole the hearing from her right ear. Three days after Christmas 1987, at 45 years of age, she woke up to find herself totally deaf from the delayed effect of the same disease.

What hindered her recovery most was not all the lifestyle adjustments required, though these were formidable enough, but "those who insisted that by going to some healing service I would be miraculously healed—or the pastor-'friend' who wanted to pray for revelation of something in my past that was hindering my healing," Naomi wrote. "They looked on it as some temporary testing by God and said we just needed to pray the right way. At the same time I was trying to accept the permanence of it. I do believe some are healed miraculously, but I felt I was not one of them, and to keep insisting that I go to some prayer meeting so they could pray for me was hindering the grief process. *They* were not accepting what I was trying to accept. When someone's husband dies and is buried, you don't pray over the wife that he'll come back—that's essentially what they were doing."

When you're in the pit, a veritable plethora of advisors will arise who think themselves qualified to tell you: "Do this; don't do that; get on with living; stop feeling sorry for yourself; don't worry, be happy"—ad nauseam.

To all of them, from all of us: *Get real.*

I Am You and You Are Me and We Are All Together

The third approach, identification, occurs when a helper, seeing Charlie's predicament, feels for the poor guy so much he jumps right into the pit with him.

Identifiers are not as easy to critique, perhaps because sympathetic friends are better than nothing. After all, if Charlie gives a pity party and nobody comes, he feels worse than he did before. If you dive into that muck with him, Charlie will feel better for awhile. But you'll both eventually drown.

Identification is one reason bars are so full; there may not be any answers beyond the anesthesia of alcohol, but at least misery has company, an essential commodity for people who have no intention of getting out of their pit because muck-treading is less threatening than having to face the unknowns of the cold, cruel world. If you're going to become an effective helper, you'll have to learn the difference between sympathy and empathy, or you'll keep getting drawn into the pit without realizing why.

If my own personal experience tells anything, sometimes people become helpers (even professional helpers) partly because of their own need to settle unresolved issues. When this is true, they gravitate toward others with problems similar to their own. If they're not careful, they end up jumping into pits with a lot of people. If they're Olympic-level helpers, they may tread muck superbly with "Charlie," maybe even set a world record, but if another helper doesn't come along and rescue them, both Charlie and his would-be helper will eventually go under.

Some people are driven into the healing professions by a need to be needed. Certainly, if these factors can affect trained professionals, you need to be aware of them, too. I want to be clear, though. I'm not denigrating caring. A little caring goes an awfully long way in helping a heartbroken friend. But here are a few questions to ask yourself:

- Do I feel driven to solve Charlie's problem for him?
- Do I feel so involved I'm being absorbed by him?
- When Charlie talks, am I mad at the things he's mad at, offended by or even bitter at the sources of his heartbreak?
- When he blames anyone or anything for making him unhappy, do I find myself in full support?
- Do the things he shares remind me of my own woes, which I then freely share with him?
- If your heartbroken friend is of a different gender than you, do you struggle with sexual desires or fantasies when

you talk together about heartbreak? If so, this may be because you need to give or receive comfort in this ultimate sense. But this solution will certainly not help your friend, because the need lies *within you*. (WARNING: Get out before you both get burned!)

- How do you feel when Charlie expresses his own doubts and fears, especially when they relate to faith and even border on blasphemy? If you're afraid, it may be that he is verbalizing the way *you feel*, but have never dared to state.

You Are You, and I Am Me ... but I Do Care

If you want to help Charlie, go get a ladder, put it into his pit, climb down and say, "Hey, friend, you're not alone. I want you to know I care and that's why I've come. I'll stay as long as it takes, but when you're ready to climb out of this muck, we'll do it together."

The main difference between sympathy and empathy is not necessarily the intensity of emotional involvement with your heartbroken friend. Your feelings may be *more intense* in empathy, for instance, when Charlie decides he's not ready to get out, even though you can see the hurt is killing him. But that's *his problem*. Yours is to find a way to love him back to life. Your reason for trying to help him is because *he needs it*, not because you have something to prove or some hole to fill in your own psyche.

It's a matter of goals, really. What is the goal of your involvement with your heartbroken friends? If you are wholeheartedly committed to helping them find their way beyond heartbreak, regardless of the personal cost to you, you have a servant-heart. This is the key element in empathetic comforting and the integrating core of loving. Although the word *servant* never occurs in the "Love Chapter," it is used elsewhere to describe what motivated Jesus to enter our heartbroken world: to heal our hurts on their own terms (and turf).

Each of you should look not only to your own interests, but also to the interests of others. Your attitude should be the same as that of Christ Jesus: Who, being in very nature God, did not consider equality with God something to be grasped, but made himself nothing, taking the very nature of a servant, being made in human likeness. And being found in appearance as a man, he humbled himself and became obedient to death – even death on a cross (Ph 2:4-8).

This was empathic love, fulfilling his own words: "Greater love has no one than this, that one lay down his life for his friends" (Jn 15:13). This empathic sacrificial love had a goal: "Let us fix our eyes on Jesus, the author and perfecter of our faith, who for the joy set before him endured the cross, scorning its shame" (Heb 12:2). The "joy" was his vision of our salvation, another word for which is *wholeness*.

When this is your only goal for your heartbroken friend, and your motive is that of a servant-friend, you have embraced the way of therapeutic loving, with its hurts as well as its joys, the only approach that can truly help your heartbroken friend.

Examples of Servant-Friendship

It's rare, but some people seem to have a special gift for helping in creative and practical ways:

- Sandra, the woman with multiple sclerosis, said: "A friend brought flowers from her garden, so I could see what was blooming. I missed all of spring, except for those flowers. People sent cards, which had never meant much to me before but suddenly conveyed caring. My husband came and fed me soup, something so unlike him. People came with food and helped clean the house. A neighbor and her husband figured out a way to wash my hair while I was on a stretcher – and came every week for months, 'til I could use the shower."
- Rachel, whose two-and-a-half-year-old son drowned in their pool, described an immobilizing grief, during which her sister even helped bathe her. Later on, she said, "I had one

Christian friend who took time to do a weekly Bible study with me, as I desired more privacy and had such personal needs. She prayed with me and for me for a year and I love her for her commitment."

- Christa, whose severely handicapped daughter lived four years, said she appreciated "people who dared to invade our defenses to play with our kids, wash our dishes, people who dared to love Ruth as Ruth, who talked and played with her, who looked beyond her lacking abilities to interact with the beautiful child within."

- Diana, after struggling with infertility, became pregnant, but miscarried. The same week she injured her back and spent seven weeks in bed, in pain and unable to function. Thirteen months later, she miscarried again. "A friend wrote down the numbers of Psalms that especially spoke to the brokenhearted and gave the list to me explaining they'd helped her," Diana said. "A friend asked me how I was feeling and then listened without telling me how I 'ought' to feel. She also did special things on days that had special significance to my pain—for example, a bag of cookies on the Sunday I returned to church. Sundays were especially painful, both due to the perennial presence of women whose babies were alive and growing and the awareness of my brokenness before God."

- Jenny, with whose story we began this chapter, had a casual friend who sent her two to three cards a month that said, "I know you hurt and I care." Another friend would come and take her shopping or to lunch. But the greatest love she experienced was from her husband. "Our counselor knelt in front of us," she said, "emphasizing that we were different and we would grieve differently and we needed to respect each other's way through this and support each other wherever we were. Our marriage, good before, is stronger now."

For Reflection or Discussion

1. After Jenny's daughter died of a self-inflicted gunshot wound, Jenny needed somebody with "love enough to carry a piece of my pain." If anyone has ever done this for you, share in a group setting whatever you feel comfortable revealing about that experience.

If several people describe what friends did for them, make a list of common themes. How is this the meaning of: "Carry each other's burdens, and in this way you will fulfill the law of Christ" (Gal 6:2)? If we are under grace, what can the "law of Christ" be?

2. Contrast Jenny's non-Christian friends, who were "there" for her, with the responses of her pastor, her Christian friend who leveled with her, and her own brother. Rate their relative effectiveness in "carrying a piece of the pain." Can you think of reasons why each "comforter" was more or less helpful? In a group setting, role-play a conversation where all parties are trying to help Jenny at the same time. Debrief afterwards, first with the "players" and then including the observers with a focus on what was, or was not, helpful.

3. Discuss the differences between the identifier and the soul mate, along with the dangers of the former style, both to the comforter and the one he is trying to help.

4. Review the "questions to ask yourself," and how each of them might keep you from falling into your friend's pit. Are there other issues to avoid, also?

5. If you sense that "identification" is taking place between another person and someone they are trying to help, how might you intervene?

6. How can empathic helping increase a helper's own pain? When this happens, what can be done about it?

7. Why are goals so crucial if we really want to help a particular friend? List some examples of goals, and discuss both the positives and negatives of each in terms of yourself and the person you wish to help.

8. As our servant, Jesus entered the heartbreak of human existence like no one before or since. List characteristics of his servant-love, using any Scriptures that come to mind, including those mentioned in the text. After creating this list, see if you can identify a pattern that someone who really wants to become a better helper might emulate.

Finally, on a personal level, choose a short-term goal in the process of change you would like to see happen in a person you wish to help. Write out a prayer that expresses both your goals and your own commitment to growth during this process. In a group setting, if participants wish to share these goals with each other, end by praying that they would become a reality.

6

Life goes on

*But sometimes your friend
will need an invitation.*

BRENDA WAS IN the kitchen when she heard the sound of the glass breaking. She ran to the family room, and there was Celeste, her six-year-old, facing away from her saying, "Momma, I think I'm cut."

Brenda's little girl had run, full tilt, into the sliding glass door, not realizing it was shut, and one of the pieces had sliced the left side of Celeste's face from her mouth back to her ear and then down her neck, barely missing her jugular vein.

"Half her face was lying down on her chest," Brenda said. "I ran over and pulled it back up in place and held it and started walking slowly backwards, talking to her, and yelling for somebody to dial the doctor.

"We called for an ambulance, but while we waited, there I was, holding Celeste, with her looking at me with these huge eyes saying, 'Momma, am I okay?'"

Finally the ambulance arrived. Celeste had lost a lot of

blood, but since her vital signs were stable, the ambulance crew didn't do much except take off for the hospital, 20 miles away, at 80 miles per hour down Ute Pass in the snow.

For Celeste, the crisis was over – several hundred stitches took care of that. For Brenda, however, it had just begun. "There was a rattle that went through my entire body – I'll never forget *the sound of my heart breaking*," she said, "before the ambulance even got there. I don't know how else to describe it.

"In the hospital there was a cleaning lady who asked what had happened," she added. "I told her Celeste had had an accident. The bandage had just been taken off that morning, and there were hundreds of sutures. That cleaning lady looked at her and said, 'Oh, didn't that ruin her!'"

Fighting for Equilibrium

The next time Brenda heard that sentiment expressed, it was from *one of her own relatives*, who said, "Maybe you're still in shock because it ruined her appearance."

Naturally, any caring mother would be worried how to help her recently disfigured daughter cope. While Brenda's relative wanted to straighten out Brenda's attitude, Brenda was worrying what she was going to say the first time the school kids called Celeste "scarface."

"When that day came," Brenda said, "all I could do was sit and rock her and cry with her. As a parent you're supposed to be able to help your kids and give them reasons and help make everything okay. But I found out sometimes that's not possible.

"The best I could do was tell Celeste that we all have scars in our lives – imperfections and flaws – and it just happens that yours will be visible all your life. We'll have to handle it together."

But the more Brenda identified with Celeste's needs, the more she distanced herself from her family and friends. This is one of the most devastating effects of a significant loss – a profound sense of separation, even dissociation, from those who should be closest to us, sometimes from life itself.

"It threw me for a loop for a long, long time," she admitted. "I couldn't pray; I couldn't sing. I went to church, but I didn't know why I was there or if I really cared anymore. My husband at that time [she's since remarried – another common result of devastating loss] was an introverted person. We had very poor communication, which I'm sure I didn't help improve. But he wasn't there at the time of the accident, and he didn't hold her face up and have the blood running all over his hands," she said. "I don't think he ever understood my feelings."

Beyond that, the very small, traditional church Brenda was attending believed that if you belong to the Lord, everything's fine: You're covered, life's wonderful, Jesus is good, and so forth. So when the accident happened they seemed to reflect: *Well, somebody's being punished.*

Brenda could never understand why a six-year-old child should have to go through the rest of her life with this kind of problem. So she withdrew to the only refuge she trusted – inside herself. She tried to be the strong mother with the right answers, but she didn't have anybody to talk to. Partly because of this isolation, Brenda slowly slid into mental illness.

"I'm sure the church group prayed for us," she said. "But nobody knew how to help me. I was locked inside myself, so ill for a long time. I begged my husband to put me in a mental institution. I contemplated suicide several times and came very close to trying it once. The mind does strange things."

Fringe People Need Somebody

Thankfully, accidents like this are relatively rare. On the other hand, Brenda – a regular Christian person I once worked with – was so surprised by this catastrophe that she got "beamed" into a very personal twilight zone, without warning and without any way to defend herself.

The reason I've told you her story is not because it's so different, however, but because it's so *similar* to the way many believers desperately try to process heartbreak—which usually sneaks up on you, as it did with Brenda, grabs you by the throat and refuses to let go.

Initially, heartbroken people simply try to cope, to survive, to somehow get beyond the crisis, as Brenda did when she pressed her daughter's face back in place as if by some superhuman effort she could glue the flesh where it should be and everything would return to normal.

For this mother, as for most survivors, normal never returns—it can't, too many factors have changed—and the main issue becomes to what degree, if at all, they will be able to adjust to the "new normal."

During this adjustment process, which can seem to take forever, "comforters" often begin in the wrong place in their attempt to help. They start with *spiritual issues*, as if some prayer or spiritual change of heart could cure a problem like the one Brenda faced. This heartbroken mother's real problem was that she desperately needed somebody to meet her where she was and invite her back into life again. But there wasn't anybody. There almost never is.

You see, Brenda wasn't just depressed, and she wasn't being selfish, as if Celeste's beauty or lack of it somehow built up or diminished her mother's ego. Yes, she was besieged with guilt for not having protected her daughter from such a calamity, but nobody in Brenda's rather typical relational circle got her point: *Something has happened here of monumental importance— to Celeste, AND to me. Our dreams have died and what I need, what I long for most, is a friend to say, "It's okay, Brenda. If I were you, I'd feel the same way. I'd have similar questions, especially in relation to God."*

What Brenda actually received was silence, distance, exile— all of which, in her psychological state, she could only interpret as judgment: "Too bad. So sad. You're bad."

Into the Wilderness

Here was a brokenhearted woman, trying to find her way through an emotional, relational and spiritual wasteland. A map and a compass might have been helpful, and perhaps that's what her church friends thought they were giving her through their exhortations. But this particular wilderness can be an intensely frightening experience if you've never been there before, or you've never even heard that such a place exists.

In some ways, Brenda was like the lost sheep in Jesus' parable of the shepherd who leaves the 99 to fend for themselves in order to search for the lost one until he finds it. When the lost one is found, the shepherd puts it on his shoulders, carries it home and then invites his friends and neighbors to a celebration.

A shepherd who really loves *all* his sheep will consistently put the recovery of *one* lost sheep ahead of the maintenance of the rest, and *rejoice more* over the recovery of that *single individual* than over the fact that the rest of the flock never strayed.

In relation to the sense of lostness that comes with a broken heart, this has significant implications for the way pastors view their responsibilities. If my perceptions are correct, most pastors focus most of their energies on the larger group for a variety of reasons including *their demand, or at least their expectation* that it will be so. When pastoral "success" is measured by growth—primarily numerical and financial—and the preacher is expected to spend 30 hours in sermon preparation and another 15 in visiting the "faithful," not to mention various other duties, those lost sheep are on their own. The message sent is, "Find your own way back to the fold."

If pastors do spend an "inordinate amount of time" seeking the lost sheep, they may be chided or worse for investing their energies in people who have little potential to contribute and who may, instead, divert resources because of their many needs.

Like the Pharisees whose indictment Jesus was answering

How to Help a Heartbroken Friend

with this parable, the consensus of the flock still may be: "She disconnected *herself*, let her find her own way back. *We* haven't moved and we'll still be here when she sees the error of her ways and decides to return."

Jesus' response was *to go looking* for the lost ones and then carry them "home" on his shoulders and celebrate. Whether it was the outcasts, the hurting, the disenfranchised, disabled, or broken, he treated them all with this kind of loving acceptance and respect. This was God's grace breaking into human experience, yet it irritated those who thought Jesus ought to pay a lot more attention to good people like themselves.

If you really want to help disconnected people, you may have to contend with attitudes like these, at the same time you'll have to risk sharing their disorientation, anxiety and sorrow – coming face to face with your own relative lostness even as you walk together, or you carry one of them, out of the wilderness. You don't have to be an ordained minister in order to do this, but you do need to fulfill the root meaning of the word *pastor*, which is "shepherd."

Pastors Need Pastors

Sometimes pastors need to be shepherded in this very same way. For a long time after Jonathan's death, I wandered in my own wilderness – lost, disconnected, isolated, wounded and broken. More than any other time in my life, I was personally, relationally and professionally at risk as I wallowed in my grief, unable and sometimes unwilling to do much of anything else.

Sometimes I wonder what it might have been like to have been visited, during those dark days, by a "pastor" who understood what I was going through. Would it have been like this?

Setting: It's late on a Saturday morning about six months after Jonathan's death. I am still in my robe, unshowered and unshaven when the doorbell rings.

Dave: Thinking: *Oh no, who can that be?* answers the door. Karl.

Oh, it's you. Come in.

Karl: Did I come at a bad time?

Dave: Yes. (Smiles) Any time is bad, you know that.

Karl: (Nods) I remember. Looks like I'm just in time for breakfast.

Dave: I was just kind of lounging around, waiting for college football to come on.

Karl: How are things going for you these days?

Dave: You need to ask? Pastors aren't supposed to think such words as come to mind.

Karl: Still pretty tough, eh?

Dave: Yup. The hard part is having to get up and preach every week and teach Sunday school and do the Wednesday night service. I just barely make it through sometimes.

Karl: I'm sure most of the people don't realize the load you are carrying right now.

Dave: They want me to carry on like nothing happened.

Karl: I know. They're thinking that it's been six months and life goes on. Things are born and things die. That's the way it works, at least on the farm.

Dave: But we're not talking about somebody's prize bull here. Jonathan was a human being, not an animal. I can't just pretend that life goes on. Life doesn't go on. At least not for me.

Karl: But how about golf? One reason I came by today is because I need a good golf partner next Saturday to play with me and a couple other guys.

Dave: (Sighs) I don't know, Karl. It's just a lot easier to stay home. I don't think I could stand being out. It's such a small town, and they're probably talking about me. I haven't been out visiting so what would they say if they knew I went golfing?

Karl: If they're talking about you, it's because they wish they could help in some way. They just don't know how.

Dave: I don't either. I thought I did, but it was just words before. Now I don't know – sometimes I don't even know what I believe any more. I feel like I'm a robot, just going through the motions.

Karl: I know what that's like. I felt that way for a long time after Eric died. But sometimes we have to get ahold of ourselves and realize we have a life to live.

Dave: Did you ever feel like dying instead?

Karl: Yes.

Dave: I'd rather die, instead.

Karl: For me, it took a conscious effort to decide I was going to get past it, going to make it. That time will come for you, too.

Dave: I don't know, man. It sure doesn't feel that way. It feels like I'm going in the other direction.

Karl: It won't happen by itself, of course. You have to make some choices. Are you sure you won't play golf with me next Saturday? You could help me keep my ball on the course.

Dave: I'm sorry. I just can't do it. Maybe another time. But thanks for asking.

Different Folks, Different Strokes

For a long time, I didn't want to get better. Brenda got lost inside herself and her husband eventually left – the cancer of unresolved issues and feelings won the battle. Everybody's different, so we all have to journey from the periphery back into the mainstream of life again in our own way and at our own pace.

I had a friend, Ed Schupbach, a pastor who did help me, though it took me years to understand how much. Ed came looking for me, just making himself available, without implying that I needed fixing and he was going to do it for me.

"You need to get away?" he would say. "I know where there's a cabin you could use."

"You want to go fishing?" he asked. "There's some pretty good places up here."

We really didn't get together enough, but Ed was a shepherd looking for a lost sheep. I don't remember a lot of what we said or what we did. What I do remember is *Ed let me be me.* He asked a lot of questions, but I think it was because he really wanted to understand what the wilderness was like. And I don't think he ever judged me if (or when) my answers were less than orthodox.

Every heartbroken person needs a friend like that. If you're going to connect with a person who's out on that periphery, you'll need a double portion of acceptance, gentleness, understanding and kindness or your beneficent intrusion may feel like pity, condescension or criticism to the person you're trying to reach.

Here are some suggestions for how to do this:

- Validate your friend's sense of disconnection. Just being accepted by somebody may help them open up even more to you.
- Be gently persistent. Your friend may not be ready this week to go to a baseball game, so don't force anything. But keep offering. Someday they'll take you up on it.
- Search for some activity to share, even if it means attending something – from an opera to a demolition derby – that you wouldn't personally choose.
- If your friend's loss was traumatic and sudden, every week for at least six months, stop in and let them know you're thinking of them. During these visits, try to discern where they are and tailor your next offer of something to do to match their status.
- If you have small children and you want to help an older widow, when the time seems right, invite her to become a surrogate grandma. One physician-friend with five kids recently asked a patient if she would like to go to the zoo with their family. The woman replied, "Oh, thank you. I'd

How to Help a Heartbroken Friend

love that. I've been feeling really lonely lately."

- Regardless of what your friends say about God or anything else, steadfastly refuse to reject them. Eventually, they will realize you have journeyed into the wasteland of their pain and they'll be much more open to walking with you out of it.
- Investigate what support groups are meeting in your area, then invite your friend *to go with you* to the one that seems to best address the need. Attend all the sessions together and use what's said there as a basis for your continuing dialogue.

For Reflection or Discussion

1. Suppose you were visiting your friend Brenda in the hospital when the cleaning woman commented on Celeste's awful scars: "Oh, didn't that ruin her!" What would you have said or done?

Has anything like that ever been said to you? If so, describe how it felt and how you responded.

2. You're visiting Brenda in her home when Celeste comes crying in the door from school saying, "Momma, they called me 'scarface'!" Answer the same questions as above.

3. Brenda said she could "hear" her own heart break. What do you think she was describing? If something like that has happened to you, try to describe it in different terms.

4. What were the causes of Brenda's mental illness? If she were your friend, how would you try to help her?

5. When they try to help, why do "comforters" often begin with their heartbroken friend's *spiritual* issues:

___ Because that's the key to everything else.

___ Because the Bible only addresses those issues.

___ Because this may, in fact, be God's judgment or discipline, and if so, somebody needs to point it out.

___ Because feeling with (or just being with) somebody is much harder than exhorting him to get right with God.

___ Other:

6. The children of Israel spent 40 years wandering in the wilderness, but God used that time to work in their lives. What are some of the parallel values of a personal "wilderness experience"?

___ To refine faith.

___ To teach dependence.

___ To clarify identity.

___ To extinguish a victim mentality.

___ All of the above.

___ Other:

7. Do you think there are pressures on your ministers that keep them from seeking and restoring the lost sheep of your congregation? If so, identify them. After making a list, brainstorm what you as a group might do to help change this.

8. Have you ever felt like a lost sheep? Try to "draw" a word picture, first, and then actually have someone do a composite sketch of this parable, using sheep and shepherd (or symbols) for all the parties involved.

9. In Jesus' day, the lepers were outcasts, yet he healed them, even touched them. As modern-day "lepers," persons with AIDS often feel like outcasts. Share any experiences you have had in trying to reconnect someone with AIDS to life. Read Matthew 8:1-4 and discuss any factors in this story that could help you relate to a heartbroken friend with AIDS.

10. How common do you think the "wedge" is between spouses after a significant loss? How does this same analogy apply to other relationships? What drives the wedge and what can you think of that might start to knock it back the other way, if it's not too late already? In a group setting, have some-

one sketch the components and dynamics of this crucial factor in heartbreak.

11. The story of David's treatment of Mephibosheth is one of the most touching pictures of kindness in the Scriptures. Read 2 Samuel 4:4 and 9:1-13 and list the ways the new king treated his potential rival as his own *kindred.*

Identify elements of David's attitudes and actions that can be universalized to any situation where a heartbroken friend needs godly kindness.

Once you have completed this list, review it, looking for parallels to the way that God has demonstrated kindness toward you. How might living with a more continual awareness of this expression of God's grace become a powerful motivator and model for you as you seek to nudge your marginalized friend back toward life again?

7

What to do when you don't know what to do

Quite often what your friend needs most is not a card or a sermon ...

ARLENE LOOKED OUT the window anxiously as the thunder from the approaching storm kept getting louder. *This one's going right over us,* she thought. *Where's Bobby?*

Her seven-year-old had been playing in the yard across the street. Arlene relaxed just a little when she noticed the kids, huddled under the trees, preparing to wait out the storm bravely as if it were just another adventure to add to their seemingly endless escapades together.

Suddenly, out of nowhere, a reddish fireball appeared in the sky, struck one of the trees, followed its trunk to the ground and disappeared with a frightening roar. For Arlene, even more alarming was a reality that took a split second to register: *Bobby? Bobby was under that tree! No!*

Arlene rushed outside, barefoot, through the mud to the adjoining yard, to find Bobby lying dead in the soft evergreen needles, his eyebrows and eyelashes burned off. She tried mouth-to-mouth resuscitation, but got no response. She didn't know how to do CPR—nobody did in those days.

There was no rescue squad, either. So Arlene sat there in shock, holding Bobby and waiting for a doctor to come, trying to convince herself, *This isn't happening. It's not real!* But every time she looked at Bobby, a different reality iced her soul.

The doctor's words confirmed what her heart rejected but her mind knew as truth. "I'm sorry," he said. "He's gone. There's nothing we can do. You should go home. I'll wait here with him and take care of everything."

Sadly, Arlene finally consented, slowly dragging herself back to her own house, wishing her husband wasn't out of town. *Have to call him. How can I tell him? How can I tell anybody? Who should I call?* She pondered these and many other unwelcome questions as she slumped heartbroken in a chair, alone.

Within an hour, however, "A neighbor lady whom I barely knew came in the house," she remembers, "and not knowing what to do or say ... she washed my feet."

Profound Simplicities

Although it's been decades since Bobby died, Arlene's most enduring positive memory from that whole horrifying experience is a simple gesture by someone who was neither a believer nor a close friend. Caring, when it connects with brokenness this directly, is more substantial than a hundred funeral sermons or a thousand cards of consolation.

Of course, we're dealing with selective recall here, and you might want to dismiss such a simple act as insignificant compared to other things that must have been said or done by pastors, Christian friends, or others who tried to help. But if Arlene's memory is anything like mine, one function of time in relation to these issues is that it sorts out what was valuable and important from what wasn't.

Pastors, especially, think our most important ministry in

situations like this is functionary – visitation, counseling, preparation and presentation of a sermon, advising or helping with or even totally handling the funeral arrangements.

But if the heartbroken people we've tried to help would level with us, we'd be both surprised and chagrined to discover what really mattered *to them* is, quite often, the way someone met a physical need.

For instance, Gerry, who pastored in a small town, is fondly remembered not so much for his many "ministerial" functions but because when there was a death in the community (not just among his parishioners) he went out, bought a ham, and took it to the family's home. "This is for you to use wherever you need it," he said. If they invited him in, fine. If they didn't he left the gift and went home. Either way, he became part of that family's permanent mental "home movie" of the events surrounding their loss.

Obviously, you don't have to be a pastor to do something like this. In fact, based on what others have told me over the years, the people who helped most were usually laypersons. Here are a few examples:

- Cindy's neighbor would often slip in the back door, take the dirty laundry home and then bring it back later, clean and neatly folded. Immediately after Cindy's husband died, this friend gathered up all the husband's soiled clothes, took them to her home, washed them and packed them in a box. About a month later she said to Cindy, "I have Bruce's things. What do you want to do with them?"

  Sometimes this woman did Cindy's dishes or cleaned the house. Often she would leave several plates of food on the counter because she knew Cindy was struggling with even simple things like feeding her children. Beyond the many practical ways that Cindy's "angel" of kindness helped, perhaps the most significant long-term component of her caring was that *it expressed love, with no strings attached.*

- Jennifer needed help during the final stages of her husband's bout with lung cancer. "Men from the church came to visit David and do household chores he couldn't do. Within the first month after David's death, some men finished projects he had started, took the trash to the dump and plowed the yard."

- Kendra and Kim were friends before Kendra's daughter died, but shortly after this event, Kim, a grandmother with a business to run, arrived at Kendra's doorstep one morning armed with deli food and a willing spirit. "We were writing thank-you notes," Kendra recalls, "and Kim came in and said, 'What can I do?' She offered to help us write, but we felt we had to do it in our own language. So after awhile, she said, 'Come on, Kendra. Let's get this house cleaned up.'"

Coming from anybody else, that offer might have offended Kendra, but coming from Kim, it didn't. "She took the time, she gave us her day, the whole day," Kendra said. "She brought lunch and ate with us. And she got me in gear as we threw some stuff in the washer. The house wasn't that despicable. She was saying, 'Come on, life goes on. Let's function.'"

Kim cared enough to drive a long distance to try to help Kendra personally cope with their loss. A phone call, card or flowers might have expressed her concern, but in person she could really see and address what needed the most attention.

Being There Is Just the Beginning

If this book has had any common theme thus far it's that *being there* when your heartbroken friend needs someone to share the pain is the most important factor in being a mender of hearts.

But if you're willing to pay the cost, being there is just part of becoming involved in some practical and personal way in addressing the unique needs inherent in every person's wilderness experience.

When the people of Israel wandered in their wilderness, waiting for the unbelieving generation to die, the Lord provided manna to eat and water to drink. Their clothing did not rot, nor did their feet swell as they traveled many, many miles in fulfilling God's program for refining their faith.

There are many lessons in this biblical example, but one that applies here is that even if your friend's desert journey is a direct judgment for a specific sin (highly unlikely, but possible), God will not abandon anyone, but will continue to provide for even the most basic needs. How can we dare do less?

Most often, God's provision is expressed through people. In the Old Testament, the prophet Elijah was sent to the widow at Zarephath to meet her needs as well as his own. It was the middle of a drought through which God was judging King Ahab, and the brook by which Elijah had been staying had dried up. When the prophet met the woman, she was gathering sticks to make a fire on which she planned to prepare the last meal for herself and her son. But because she was faithful enough first to make from her meager supply of flour and (olive) oil a meal for Elijah, the Lord never let her jar of flour or jug of oil run dry until the rains came again and both her needs and Elijah's were met during that entire time. In effect, God provided for each of them through the other (see 1 K 17:1-16).

Elijah's successor, Elisha, was also God's instrument to meet the physical needs of another widow who was in desperate straits. Her husband, one of the "company of the prophets," had died, and now their creditor was coming to take the woman's two sons as his slaves.

All this heartbroken woman had left in her house was a little bit of oil. Elisha told her to borrow empty jars from all her neighbors. "Don't ask for just a few," he instructed her. "Then go inside and shut the door behind you and your sons. Pour oil into all the jars."

After all the jars were filled, the miraculous flow of oil stopped. The widow sold the oil, paid her debts and still had enough left over for her and her sons to live on. The point: God is concerned with more than "spiritual" needs. He takes a personal interest in our physical needs, many of which he meets through other people (see 2 K 4:1-7).

In the New Testament, Jesus often addressed physical needs. His very first miracle, when he turned water to wine so the wedding celebration at Cana could continue, is testimony enough that the Lord's interests went far beyond merely saving souls. He fed the 5,000 because they were hungry. He healed untold numbers – the blind, the lame, the deaf, the lepers, and many others – because *they were better off well*. Of course, in each case, there was a spiritual lesson, but from the perspective of those healed, the main lesson was that Jesus cared enough to apply his miraculous power at the point of their physical need.

The strongest indictment of the early church's neglect of people in need was made by James, the half-brother of Jesus, perhaps because he had seen the Lord in action. "What good is it, my brothers and sisters," he asks, "if you say you have faith but do not have works? Can faith save you? If a brother or sister is naked and lacks daily food, and one of you says to them, 'Go in peace; keep warm and eat your fill,' and yet you do not supply their bodily needs, what is the good of that?" (Jm 2:14-16).

In one confrontation with the teachers of his day (see Mk 7:9-13), Jesus pointed out the hypocrisy of religion that lacked a heart for people's real needs, even the needs of one's own father and mother. Even though the Law commanded, "Honor your father and mother," the religious tradition nullified this if what might have been available to help them had been promised to God instead.

The result was that because of someone's vows, their religious teachers *would not allow them to help their parents*. The conflict here is not just between interpretations of the Law. The basic issue is the separation of physical and spiritual realities, or the secular and the sacred. In Jesus' view, even when a person had promised their present (and future) excess financial resources to God – a commendable spiritual act in itself – meeting the needs of their aging parents still took precedence.

James was concerned that the church might slide backwards toward the attitude that spiritual issues are all that matter. Sometimes this perspective still drives people when it comes to helping the heartbroken among us. Thankfully, however, some heart-menders understand the crucial importance of addressing more practical needs, too.

Help When I Needed It Most

Several bereaved parents described practical help that had a long-term impact:

- Sharlene's two-year-old son Jesse died after struggling with cancer. During this ordeal, Sharlene's church friends were a real godsend. "My friends and church family were a continual support," she wrote. "There was nothing anyone could *say* that made me feel better; however, what people *did* helped more than anything. When I was unable to function properly, someone would bring a meal, clean or help with my other child. Keeping my home in a functioning order was so important to me, but I was unable to do it.

  "My heart breaks for people who don't have a pastor or church like we have," she said. "Our pastor was our friend – and constantly was there for us. We also had 'deacon care groups.' Our deacon and his wife made many trips to the hospital with us. He even went so far as to pack his office work into a briefcase and take us to Philadelphia for Jesse's tests. He waited and did his work all day and was there for us when we needed him most.

  "In our church we also have a lady who plans meals for anyone coming home from the hospital. We always had a meal waiting when we came home from a long day of chemotherapy."

- Andrea was driving the car when it slid off an icy road and into a telephone pole, killing her six-year-old, Jamie. "One close friend became our 'chauffeur' and drove us to the funeral home, the florist, etc., that whole week when we were unable to think straight," Andrea wrote. "Someone else organized meals to be brought to us for several weeks. At the reviewal, our 'chauffeur' and his wife brought us water and encouraged us to take breaks when things got too emotionally draining."

  Writing only four months after the tragedy, Andrea added, "A few very faithful friends have continued to express concern and love by listening (most important) and by calling us instead of waiting for us to call them. It was Jamie's birthday this time – three people sent plants or flowers and many remembered by sending a 'Thinking of you' card. Ashley, our four-year-old daughter, has received a letter or package every week for these past four months from her aunt and cousin who have tried in many ways to establish a real closeness and bond with her, for siblings seem to get lost in the shuffle."

- Wendy had two miscarriages in a row after trying for years to conceive, but some people, including family members, didn't seem to want to acknowledge her sense of loss as legitimate.

  "It was only with the people who made the effort to come to our home that we truly let go and sought comfort," she wrote. "Over the phone, we tried much harder to be brave and put up a good front. With a real, live person in front of us, we were more able to receive comfort. It's almost as if the family members who couldn't get in the car and drive 30 minutes were silently saying the event wasn't all that catastrophic."

  Based on her experience, to comfort someone facing a similar loss, Wendy would "be on their doorstep in a flash, with something highly caloric. I'd make a date once a week or so for the first month just to see how they're doing," she wrote. "I'd also make a note of when the event occurred (if practical) and let them know on that date that I realize how hard the anniversary must be."

Laying Up Treasures in Heaven

Sometimes the heartbroken friend we're trying to help may be dying. In this case, it's not so much a question of recovery as something else – coping, preparation, or even simply saying good-bye.

- Brenda's cousin Francine had been diagnosed with leukemia. Just before Francine was to begin chemotherapy, she asked Brenda, "Would you go to the nurses' station, get a pair of scissors and cut my hair? I'd rather have you cut my hair real short so I'll look nice for a little while before the chemo makes it all fall out."

   "I was behind her as I gave her a haircut," Brenda admitted, "and I'm sure I cried a million tears in those snips. But it's what she wanted, and if it meant that much to her to have me cut her hair instead of just having it fall out in globs, then that's what I wanted to do ... but it hurt!

   "After Francine came home I asked, 'Do you want to go see the kids' ball games?' At first, she seemed afraid to say, 'Yeah,' because it was risky for her. She never knew when she might start vomiting. But she knew I was willing to take her. The only thing that mattered for me was that I wanted to make a difference for her, because there was an end coming in her life.

   "So we'd go to the ball game and huddle up in a blanket and sometimes she would say, 'I've got to go,' and she might start throwing up on the way to the truck. But we'd get home and she would say, 'I just loved that. Seeing the kids play ball just meant so much to me.'

   "It was one of those rare times, when you can really give somebody a special gift," Brenda said.

- Mary's friend Linda, gorgeous and in her early forties, was dying of cancer. "She was one of the most beautiful Christians I've ever known," Mary said. "I wondered, *What can I do for Linda in these last months? How can I help her?*

"I decided that once a week I would offer to pick her up and take her for a ride. I made it clear she could say anything she wanted to. 'I want you to tell me if you're angry. When your hair falls out from the treatment, I want you to talk about it.'

"She did. She opened up and we would just park under a shade tree somewhere and stay as long as she wanted to, until she told me she was tired and needed to get back to bed. During those months, Linda unloaded all her feelings as we talked about whatever was on her mind.

"We even talked about her husband. 'I know Don will marry again soon, because he's just not the type that will be alone,' she said once. 'But that bothers me.' So we talked about that openly and freely. We also talked about her children, some of whom weren't Christians–a deep concern for her.

"'What are they going to do with my things, Mary?' she asked me once. It was a precious time together, and we became closer than we had been before. Toward the end one day I said, 'Linda, I have a favor to ask of you. If you get to heaven before I do, please tell Minny I love her.'"

Of course, Linda agreed, and in the end, Mary and Linda helped each other.

Helper's Checklist to Meet Physical Needs

Perhaps the best question to ask yourself in relation to addressing physical needs is: "If Jesus were here, what would he do?" When you try to address these physical needs, you become a physical link between God's comfort and the person who needs it. You could accomplish a lot less than that. Many do. But you could never accomplish more.

Once you've resolved to become that link between God and your heartbroken friend, you may still need some suggestions for how to help. Here are a few ideas to get you started:

___ hugs all around, unless this makes the huggee uncomfortable;

___ clean house, but never betray your trust by telling others how dirty things are (or anything else you observe there);

___ help write thank-you cards, especially the generic type that don't require a personal touch;

___ financial gifts, especially if the expenses are great (start a special fund if appropriate);

___ provide for child care or respite care, whichever is needed most;

___ send flowers or some personalized gift if you can't be there;

___ use your sphere of influence to address a unique need (for instance, arrange a lower airline fare);

___ ban from your vocabulary: "Call me if you need something," as this puts pressure on the one in need, who may wish not to be a burden to anyone;

___ offer to be a chauffeur, especially if your friend is in shock—you could save their life and protect others, too;

___ envision or discern what needs doing by asking, "What would I need to have done for me in this situation?" Then be sure it gets done;

___ offer legal or financial advice if you are qualified. Handling an estate or filing an income tax form can be formidable tasks for some people;

___ pastors might develop a specific checklist for newly bereaved persons to help them identify what to expect from as many directions as possible. (But don't forget to take the ham, too!)

For Reflection or Discussion

1. Can caring that connects directly with brokenness (as when Arlene's muddy feet were washed by her friend) be "more substantial than a hundred funeral sermons or a thousand cards of consolation"?

___ No doubt, though I've never experienced it.

___ I wonder, since the Truth is what really sustains anybody.

___ Consolation cards can express caring.

___ What is this, "Care Bear" theology?

2. If every heartbroken family has a permanent mental home movie of the events surrounding a loss, how would you as a helper want to be recalled?

3. The practical help that Cindy's friend provided was an expression of "love without strings attached." Review 1 Corinthians 13:4-7 for aspects of love that ought to come in this form and compare this "love without strings" to the earlier phrase "love without wax." Bring in other Scripture passages that illuminate this idea, and then, in a group setting, discuss the relative difficulty of giving or receiving this kind of love.

4. Prioritize the following list in terms of *long-term relative importance* to a church family when faced with a tragic death:

___ Picking the right funeral hymns.

___ That the funeral message includes the gospel.

___ Keeping track of – and thanking – those who send flowers.

___ Making sure the deceased's attire is nicely pressed.

___ Trying to remember what's happening next.

___ A hug and some shared tears from a friend who cares.

___ Having prepared food delivered to the home, at least once a day for a week (a month would be better), with cooks' names clearly marked on the bottom of each bowl, and with someone other than the recipient responsible for returning them.

___ That the pastor came by late one night just to see how they were doing, and to pray with them.

___ That the sermon answered all the "Why" questions.

___ That the pastor, organist and soloist all got paid.

5. One word for the Holy Spirit is *paraklete*—one called alongside (to help). In what ways might the Spirit's helping be expressed physically, as compared to the way we usually think of it?

6. The prophet Elijah experienced many miracles, not the least of which were two that involved God's meeting his physical needs. Read 1 Kings 17:1-6 and 1 Kings 19:1-9 and list not only the provisions of God, but also the needs addressed by each provision. What does this divine help reveal about the extent to which God's interest in people goes beyond what we normally call "spiritual"?

7. Writing from prison, the apostle Paul asked his young friend Timothy for help. Read 2 Timothy 4:9-22, listing the various types of needs being expressed. Compose a modern version of this passage, beginning with the phrase, "These past few years have been heartbreaking in some ways, but ... "

8. Read Mark 7:6-13 and then in a group setting have volunteers role-play a conversation involving a person with aging parents who need assistance, and the pastor of the church to which the person has pledged all their excess resources toward the multimillion-dollar building program. In the middle of the argument, if there is one, have someone representing Jesus' point of view come in and arbitrate.

9. At the end of this chapter, pastors are encouraged to develop a checklist for newly bereaved persons to help them anticipate many of the things they will face. In a group setting, create the kind of checklist you would find most helpful in this situation. When you have identified the basic issues to be addressed, ask your pastors if they would like to have a copy.

8

Somebody to hold me

*Sometimes the best answer
can't be put into words.*

ROCKY WAS A long distance runner. Many times a year his long legs propelled his slender six-foot, nine-inch frame up the grueling twelve-mile-long Pikes Peak highway and back down in less than four hours. A construction worker acquainted with hard labor, Rocky had his life changed in an instant in the 1980s when he leaned over to pick up something and a disc ruptured, injuring his spinal cord. Suddenly, Rocky was paralyzed below the waist and his family became penniless in no time because the injury wasn't job-related.

For weeks all Rocky could do, while his wife was out working, was lie in bed. He couldn't even use his own bathroom, so since they lived in the country, he would drag himself outside to use his backyard for a toilet, then back indoors to bed.

During this process, he not only lost touch with his legs, he lost touch with God. He felt abandoned and betrayed and very confused ... except when his faithful friend Glenn would visit.

"When Glenn came to see me," Rocky said, "there wasn't anything he could say. He didn't preach any sermons or tell me how I should be feeling or what I should be thinking. Instead, he would actually climb into the bed with me, wrap his arms around me and we would both cry. After he had been there, I felt like I had been bathed in love."

Rocky's issues were common to every heartbroken person who's ever lived, most of them starting with the word, "Why?" But his most helpful answer came not in words, ideas, insights or counsel, but in the form of a *person*. Somebody to hold him.

Betsy's husband was a pastor – before his adultery brought the loss of job, church and friends – for Betsy, not just for David. As a result, Betsy struggled with low self-esteem and other emotional issues that often accompany heartbreak.

Betsy wrote that she had a few friends at first, "... who would hang in despite my bizarre behavior and the things I said, not demanding that I be rational, reasonable, immediately forgiving, not angry." She also had a pastor-friend who sat with her "long enough so that one day God showed the pastor a degree of the pain of rejection I was experiencing [and] they understood."

Despite her strong personal faith, Betsy resented almost any Scripture because, she said, "I wanted Christ in the form of people to show me they cared." For a long while, Betsy became "deeply depressed as the current pain hooked back into a childhood of abuse – emotional and sexual. During this time," she recalled, "I would see only four or five people outside my nuclear family."

Betsy's magnified emotional pain fueled this depression. One pastor observed that she was hurting other people by her depressed behavior and that she should "pull herself together."

Within this brokenhearted woman was a frightened, bewildered child who needed this reassurance: *Even though life has dealt you an awful disappointment, things will be okay again.* But in order for these words of consolation to connect with Betsy's inner child, they had to be expressed in terms even a little girl could understand.

Insights, principles, even biblical truths were not very helpful when Betsy's anguish was compounded by the shame, guilt and worthlessness gushing to the surface from her underground pool of hurtful memories. With her spiritual background, Betsy already *knew all she needed to know* in order to survive, with or without the help of her friends. What she really needed was somebody to hold her – metaphorically and even physically.

Hide or Seek

Now let's suppose for a moment you are Betsy's friend (or Rocky's) and you want to help them recover more quickly and more completely than either can manage alone. Your main question will be how much emotional energy you are willing to invest. Most Christian "comforters" appeal first to the mind – we'll talk more about that next chapter – but only a *person* can bind up another person's broken heart. Only a person can find the pathway into a friend's real need, enter it and share the pain until *they* decide it's time to move beyond it.

Be warned: You can't do this alone or you'll risk being overwhelmed when your friend's pain *taps into your own emotions or memories.* You'll need help, divine help. As Betsy said, and as Glenn demonstrated, *Christ in you* will demonstrate that he and you really do care. If you've been around the church much, you've heard this idea before. But in order to transform it from a concept to reality, let's look at just one example of how Jesus showed a heartbroken friend he cared.

The friend was Peter, whose denial and restoration is one of the most gripping narratives in the Gospels. Peter, the impetuous, impulsive disciple, had promised Jesus, "Even if I have to die with you, I will never disown you."

But after the disciple's third denial, Luke says that "the Lord turned and looked straight at Peter. Then Peter remembered the word the Lord had spoken to him.... And he went outside and wept bitterly" (Lk 22:61-62).

No half-hearted remorse here. The rugged fisherman had failed as miserably as he could possibly manage. His heart was as broken as it could be.

The next time we see Jesus and Peter together, we discover that Peter had gone back to fishing and taken some of the others with him. After they had fished all night and caught nothing, the resurrected Jesus called to them from the shore and told them to cast their net on the right side of the boat. As a result they caught so many fish they couldn't even haul in the net. Peter, realizing it was the Lord, jumped overboard and waded ashore—a rather dramatic response. But something far more dramatic took place after breakfast.

> Jesus said to Simon Peter, "Simon son of John, do you truly love [*agape*] me more than these?"
>
> "Yes, Lord," he [Peter] said, "you know that I love [*phileo*] you."
>
> Jesus said, "Feed my lambs."
>
> Again Jesus said, "Simon son of John, do you truly love [*agape*] me?"
>
> He answered, "Yes, Lord, you know that I love [*phileo*] you."
>
> Jesus said, "Take care of my sheep."
>
> The third time he said to him, "Simon son of John, do you love [*phileo*] me?"
>
> Peter was hurt because Jesus asked him the third time, "Do you love me?"
>
> He said, "Lord, you know all things; you know that I love [*phileo*] you."
>
> Jesus said, "Feed my sheep" (John 21:15-17).

The basic lesson in this interchange isn't primarily analytical, semantic, or even theological. It's emotional. The resurrected Jesus is reinstating his fallen friend, giving him a new sense of mission—to shepherd the flock of God.

Since Jesus could have accomplished this in any way, at any time, and in any place he wished, the setting, method and words are very significant. He chose the *setting* where Peter was most competent – fishing – to demonstrate that the only way to succeed even in one's arena of competence is with divine guidance. The *method* matched Peter's denials, in reverse. And in his choice of *words* Jesus matched emotion for emotion, switching from his own word for love (*agape*) to Peter's (*phileo*) as if to accept the best Peter could manage at that moment. His unspoken message: "Peter, I know you don't *agape* me now, but I know that someday you will because I forgive you, and I believe in you. When you have recovered, you will strengthen your brothers."

Peter was hiding from his calling – because of his shame – so *the Lord came seeking him.* That's the way it's been between God and humans since the Garden of Eden and that's the way it will be until Jesus comes again. He simply will not let the members of his family languish in their pain without letting them know, from without or within, that he loves them.

And when he finds the one he seeks, he enters through *the open door* – in most cases, the emotions. He meets Peter on his own turf and terms, and addresses the broken man's felt need – guilt – as a way to approach a deeper need, the real need – reconciliation, renewal and recommissioning.

If you're going to help your heartbroken friend, you'll never miss if you follow this method. Make contact first with the emotions, then the mind, then the will and ultimately the spirit. Then support them until what's happening inside works its way out.

Shame – the Blight of Broken Hearts

There may be several reasons why my own recovery after Jonathan's death took so long, but a primary contributor was that I never had *somebody to hold me* in the way I've been describing. As a father I had failed. The little boy entrusted to me had died and nothing anybody could say made any real difference.

In late August, 1978, this image etched itself into the pages of my emotional self: It's the middle of the night and Jonathan, almost four, is standing on the little stool with his name on it, trying to throw up into the bathroom sink. For three days he's been nauseated – presumably a viral illness:

"Can I have a drink, Daddy?" he asks.

"Not yet, Jon," I say. "It might make you throw up again."

I didn't know any better. I told him what I'd always heard. How was I supposed to know that the next morning he would experience brain damage from dehydration and as a result of that, five weeks later he would die?

I, who would have died defending him against any and all threats to his life, became the means to his death; at least that's the way it felt and *how it felt was all that mattered* for months after the event that broke my heart.

Doctors said it wasn't my fault. Friends, family, everybody who knew about it assured me that they wouldn't have handled it differently. I tried to assume myself that I had done the best I knew how. But even if an angel from God had appeared announcing my absolution, I wouldn't have accepted it. Guilt, especially the rather abject variety experienced by bereaved parents, wraps its icy tentacles around broken hearts and refuses to yield to reason, religion or anything in between.

On one level, I functioned. I had to. There were sermons to preach, classes to teach, weddings (and funerals) to perform, babies to dedicate and people to counsel and lead to the Lord. But regardless of how good I became at using my own heartbreak to connect with other people's pain, I couldn't disconnect from my own. I could even help people gain freedom from their own guilt and shame, but I could not set myself free.

Everything I did became another opportunity to be guilty, as I pursued myself through the shadowy pathways of my own mind, constantly trying, convicting and sentencing the villain to the only thing he deserved – torment (actually, he deserved to die, but torment was the closest I could come). If I broke the

How to Help a Heartbroken Friend

speed limit, I debated turning myself in. In relation to certain other infractions, I actually did turn myself in, paying one fine. Gradually during this time I sank into the quicksand of striving to live as "righteously" as I could, not so much to prove anything as to protect myself from further self-imposed penance. As the real (but unresolved) guilt I felt about having failed Jonathan attached itself to other things, I became an obsessive-compulsive person (obsessed with my self-mortification and compelled to try to release the guilt somehow). I could tell you about the hand-washing and the doing, undoing and doing again that anyone who's been there would recognize.

Perhaps one example will suffice. Early one morning I drove past a house and the thought hit me that the smoke I saw might be from a fire. I drove a little further, assuring myself that this was highly unlikely, but then *I had to go back*, to be certain, as much for the good of the people in that house as to protect myself from the possible guilt of not having intervened to save their lives. Even after I was sure it was only chimney smoke, I still had to go back again. And then, after everything was said and done, I chastised myself for not having the willpower to stifle the impression in the first place or to keep myself from returning even when I knew better.

I was probably within an eyelash of insanity as I tried to protect my damaged emotions by not doing any more "bad" things. But no matter what standards I set, I failed, because had I achieved "perfection" for one day – which never happened – I would have chastised myself for setting my standards too low, or taken pride in my achievement, an even more despicable outcome.

The sad fact was, I *needed to fail*. Success – any success – would have been too kind an outcome for as negligent a father as I. So, I spent a lot of my time apologizing – for actions, inactions, motives, attitudes – because I so desperately needed people telling me I was forgiven. Yet no number of such assurances ever released me from my own emotional prison, designed, constructed and maintained by a brutal jailer – me.

Looking back, I wonder what would have happened if somebody had stepped into that cell with me and said, "I love you, Dave, and it breaks my heart to see the downward spiral of your struggle with guilt. If you want me to, I'll climb up on the church steeple and proclaim to the world: David's not guilty. Not guilty. NOT GUILTY! He didn't kill Jonathan. It was an accident!

"You see, Dave, that's what you've been forcing us all to do for months now and I'd do it *for years* if it would really help. But you're not listening. We could declare your innocence until we were blue in the face, and you would refuse to let go of your guilt.

"So, let's look at this another way. Maybe, just between us two, we should face something: You *are* guilty. You let Jonathan down. You failed. That's what you really feel, isn't it? That's what you believe is true. So I'm going to sit here and cry with you about that and feel this as much as any man can share another man's heartache. And when there aren't any more tears, there's one other thing I hope you will accept: I forgive you, friend. You are forgiven."

Deadly Directions

Unfortunately, no interchange like this ever took place. Nobody ever really met me where I was, at least not for years. And even then, *nobody let me be guilty so I could be forgiven.* Instead, the emotional confusion led to a deep and lengthy depression, beginning with unrelieved sadness and leading to chronic depletion (emotional, physical and spiritual) which only finally was resolved with medical intervention.

Not everyone who experiences a severe loss moves from normal grieving to real depressive illness. In fact, as Dr. George Nichols wrote in a letter to me, "Although grief is a highly individual and personal matter, most people recover slowly without special attention or treatment. It is only occasionally

How to Help a Heartbroken Friend

that a true depressive illness interrupts that recovery. The distinction is important because clinical depression can be fatal, and because it is highly curable with medical care and medicine.

"It is easy to spot a broken leg," he continued, "but recognizing a depressive illness requires a little new knowledge, usually a little change in viewpoint, and the willingness to ask a few questions – questions that bring out the signs which determine whether a person has a depressive illness or not."

Dr. Nichols speaks from experience. His youngest son committed suicide, after which the doctor dedicated himself to raising public awareness of this very common and unnecessarily deadly disease. His insights, published in the *Journal of the Christian Medical and Dental Society*, are my foundation for these "diagnostic" questions, which are not intended to replace a medical evaluation, but to assist you in determining how seriously your friends are troubled, since they may desperately need your intervention:

- How have you been feeling?
- Is anything really bothering you?
- Have you been out lately?
- What did you have for supper last night?
- When was the last time you laughed?
- Heard any good jokes lately?
- Any health problems you've never had before?

Be very sensitive to these symptoms:

- Recurrent thoughts of death or suicide
- Sad, unhappy mood; but sometimes irritable and anxious (some people deny mood changes)
- Feelings of hopelessness, worthlessness and self-reproach
- Crying or inability to cry
- Withdrawal
- Loss of interest and of pleasure in things
- Neglect of personal appearance
- Difficulty in thinking and concentrating

- Sleeping problems: may have trouble falling asleep but often awakens too early or sleeps too much
- Change in appetite or weight
- Physical: slow and tired or may be agitated and restless
- Complaints of physical ill health: e.g., fast heartbeat, headache, constipation, chronic pain (symptoms like these are common, but misleading, and disguise the underlying sadness; they probably mean they are worried about themselves and are asking for help in approved – nonemotional – words.)

Most of us have some of these symptoms at times. But if your heartbroken friend has them in combinations, or if they persist, the best help you can offer is to encourage a doctor's visit, and offer to go along. This is *extremely urgent* – in other words, refuse to take no for an answer – if the following signs are also present:

- Increasing distance and withdrawal from family and friends;
- Absence of hope;
- Hearing voices and other disordered thinking;
- Talking of suicide;
- Giving away prized possessions – e.g., trophies, hi-fi and sports equipment, baseball cards; "I won't be needing these anymore";
- Putting affairs in order – e.g., returning long-borrowed items; final contact (unspoken good-byes) with important friends and relatives;
- Sudden improvement (no longer painfully undecided).[1]

Immediate intervention is crucial if you want to help your friend *survive*, much less recover. If you really care, you'll reach out and say, "I love you and because I do we're going to the doctor to get some help for what's got you down."

When I was about as low as I ever got, a physician-friend said, "I've known you for quite awhile, Dave, but I've never seen you this down. Maybe you should consider medication;

specifically, Prozac."

I couldn't deny the depression, though I doubt I knew how bad it was. And I did trust Bob, even if I resented his intrusion, but still I resisted, probably because of the stigma of needing the pharmacological crutch. I told him I would follow up when I got home, but I battled it for several more months until pneumonia drained my last reserves and I had no other choice but to use every crutch I could find if I ever wanted to be whole again.

That was April 1991 and the one symptom I remember that seems to symbolize everything else was that even the sound of the birds singing outside each morning that spring – 13 years after Jonathan died – irritated me. The next spring I actually enjoyed their music. Hopefully, every spring that follows will increase my ability to experience nature's music as the symphony it really is, rather than the cacophony I heard in 1991 when it was still hard to believe that I would ever again be anything but sad.

(Note: See *New Light on Depression* for a comprehensive Christian discussion of depression – its symptoms, causes, treatments – including many practical suggestions about how to recognize it and help someone with this disorder.)

For Reflection or Discussion

1. Most of Rocky's emotionally laden questions began with Why? In a group setting, make a list of what these questions might have been.

2. Glenn's answer to Rocky's agony was to hold him and cry with him. Why might some potential comforters be uncomfortable with this approach? What dangers or benefits can you identify?

3. In a group setting, have someone represent Betsy, who has withdrawn in depression from just about everybody. Have one of Betsy's former friends visit her with the goal of convincing her that her reaction is a bad witness. After the visit is over, let the role players express their feelings about the interaction and then discuss as a group what might have been more helpful. Having done this, have another volunteer visit the same "Betsy" and offer her some true support.

4. What do you think of Betsy's desire for "Christ in the form of people to show me they cared"?
__ Impossible
__ Unreasonable
__ Unlikely
__ Possible, but difficult
__ Natural
__ Piece of cake
__ Other:

5. Have you ever experienced an extreme emotional reaction because the event in question has tapped some hurtful memory? If so, and you wish to do so, share it in a group setting. How might your friends help you toward healing of that memory?

6. If many believers know all they need to know in order to survive, why do so many of them suffer so deeply with

heartbreak?

___ It's part of being human.

___ It's disobedient and only makes things worse.

___ Ideas aren't very helpful in times like that.

___ Heartbreak is a lonely road.

___ Nobody cares enough to help them.

7. If you've experienced heartbreak, what approach did people use to try to help you?

8. Why is the idea of entering "the emotional open door" so crucial if you want to really connect with your hurting friend? Discuss how to find these open doors.

9. If your friend is struggling with guilt, even though nobody else puts blame on them for what has happened, would it help to say, "Okay, maybe you are guilty, but I forgive you"? How would you go about it? What dangers might there be in this approach? (Hint: If your friend is suicidal, it probably won't help much to remind them that they are guilty.)

10. Review the symptoms of depression described in this chapter and develop your own questions to discern whether your friend is depressed. If so, what might you do to try to help?

11. For believers, is there a stigma attached to seeing a psychiatrist for depression? How about taking medication for treatment of depression? In a group setting, if the group's consensus is yes to either of these, discuss why this may be true and what a more helpful attitude might be. How might even subtle agreement with this affect your ability to really help a depressed friend?

12. Choose one of the following passages and discuss how Jesus entered the person's "open door" of need:

___ The woman at the well (Jn 4:7-26)

___ The adulterous woman (Jn 8:1-11)

___ Lazarus resurrected (Jn 11:1-45)
___ The road to Emmaus (Lk 24:13-35)
___ Mary in the garden (Jn 20:11-18)

13. Draw three intersecting circles on the board, labeling them emotions, mind and will. For the purpose of discussion, let this diagram represent the personality (or soul). What are the implications of the intersections in relation to helping a person recover?

14. What emotions does God have? If we are made "in God's image," does that include an emotional component of our personality?

15. List all the emotions of Jesus you can find in the Gospels such as anger, discouragement, confusion, grief, depression, joy. Are there any hidden values to being an emotional person? How can you help a heartbroken friend capitalize on these?

16. Based on the biblical survey of God's emotions you've just done, how would you compare the way human emotions are presented in the Bible:
___ normal and natural
___ a hindrance to spirituality
___ an avenue to closeness with God
___ neutral
In light of this, how would you evaluate the Christian teaching you've received about emotions?

9

To tell the truth

Give your friend the
freedom to not pretend

LIKE MANY ALCOHOLICS, Billy Simpson started drinking heavily when he was in college. The university's football team was exciting to watch, so Billy and his friend John had to get to the stadium at least three hours before game time just to get a seat in the student section.

To pass the time, they smuggled in alcohol – starting with a pint they would share. Gradually, they needed more booze to get the same buzz. By the time they quit going to football games together, Billy and John were packing three quarts of hard liquor to every game.

Billy Simpson dropped out of college halfway through his sophomore year, moved home and got a job reading meters – which he did for many years. He also married his first wife Donna as soon as she finished high school.

Billy and Donna partied, drank, did drugs and got along reasonably well for about a year – until Donna became pregnant. Billy was unwilling to face the responsibilities of a family, so he turned increasingly to drinking and womanizing.

Like many alcoholics, Billy Simpson had a Jekyll and Hyde personality when he was drinking. "I could be talking to a friend, being completely normal, in front of a store," he said, "and the next minute kick in the window and take things out."

When Billy's first marriage ended in divorce, he married his second wife, Shelly, *the very next day*. "It was good for maybe six months," he said. "Then the same pattern returned. I started going out on her and drinking more, mainly at home, from about 5:30 p.m. until I passed out between 12:30 and 1 a.m."

Finally, Shelly convinced Billy to see a doctor, who at 75 had seen many men like Billy. "He ran a batch of tests," Billy said, "and told me I was an alcoholic. My liver was about shot and a lot of my bodily functions were starting to shut down.

"'If you don't quit,' he told me, 'you're going to kill your-self.'"

Shelly wouldn't let Billy kill himself. Two months later, Billy entered a program and he stayed sober for about a year, but on their wedding anniversary he had a couple of drinks with dinner, six or more the next day and a whole quart on the third. He stopped drinking again when Shelly warned, "I've had it with you. If you mess up again, you're out of here. I'll give you one more chance."

This time Billy stayed on the wagon for 15 months, but he always knew he would drink again someday if only to test Shelly's limits. The final episode lasted nearly four months until on New Year's Day Shelly told Billy they were finished.

Although it took her several months to get him out of the house, Billy finally got the point. He's been sober ever since, not so much by his own power, but because, as he tried to recover from his second marriage failure, someone introduced him to Christ.

At a church's divorce recovery workshop, he met Brenda (whose daughter Celeste cut her face – see ch. 6). Billy and Brenda have built a new life together in which Billy's grandchildren don't even know the person he once was but only the person he is becoming with God's help and Brenda's support. Today, because he regrets the misery he caused so many when he was drinking, Billy tries to help others in similar straits face and deal with the truth of their lives before they create their own legacy of broken hearts.

No Corner on Denial

If you were raised in the church as I was, you may think the Billy Simpsons of the world are "out there" somewhere. Not very often do people stand up *in church* (like they do in A.A.) and say, "My name is Billy and I'm an alcoholic, but, thank God, I've stopped running from the pain."

Yet Billy's journey is similar to that of many broken-hearted believers – not because they choose alcohol as an escape, but because *they choose denial in one form or another as a way of coping with their disappointments.*

Encouraged by a group of codependents who tell each other only what they want to hear when adversity happens (to reduce *their own* anxiety), the typical heartbroken Christian processes the pain in one of the following ways:

- Stoicism – This doesn't really hurt.
- Masochism – Hurting is good for me.
- Quietism – Who am I to question the will of God?
- Activism – I will rise above this.

When people aboard an airplane experience motion sickness, what they really need to do is throw up. By analogy, when travelers on the journey of faith experience vertigo, they are either told the turbulence isn't really that bad or they are handed a scopolamine patch so they won't remember it or a Dramamine tablet so they won't feel it. Seldom do they receive what they really need – a spiritual airsickness bag.

Jeremy and Toni (see ch. 3) spent years trying to find somebody who would let them be who they were so they could become what they wanted to be. "Many who come to the church do not find healing because the problems they bring do not yield easily to current ideas about victory in Christ and so they tend to be ignored," Jeremy wrote. "My heart aches for the multitudes that the church has been unable to help. The first great enemy to lasting change is our propensity to turn our eyes away from the wound and pretend things are fine. *This, to me, is lying about the truth!* The work of restoration cannot begin until a problem is fully faced.

"There is a journey we must undertake if we are to become fully healed of a painful, ugly past," he continued. "The journey involves bringing the wounded heart before God, a heart that might be full of rage, overwhelmed with doubt and unable to fellowship intimately with God. It does not seem possible that anyone (even God) can handle, let alone embrace, such a wounded and sinful heart. But the pathway to healing involves the risk of putting into words the condition of our inner being and placing those words before God for God's response."

Going Through it to Get Beyond it

After the doctors detected brain damage in our second son, Christopher, I cried out from the depths of my soul, "If that's the way it's going to be, then God can go to h---." Some believers through the years have viewed my outburst as blasphemous. I think it was the cry of a brokenhearted child trying to verbalize to his God a hurt that almost defied words. Only a few hours later, this gracious God shined the light of his hope into the darkness of my despair when I realized that God had already gone to hell, in the person of Jesus, to redeem this fallen world of which my sons' illnesses are a part and to redeem a fallen person who would dare to utter such a phrase.

Looking back, that kind of truthful interchange – me with God and vice versa – was what brought me through the experience and made me stronger. In fact, my verbal transparency before God, which on the level of words may sound outrageous to the human ear, on another level became evidence to me that our relationship was secure enough that I could risk telling God whatever I needed to.

If I had played the denial game, including saying and doing only the "right" things, I might have consigned myself to a prison of bitter resentment, ruining any chance that I would be able to fulfill what I now see as my calling: "to make a defense to every one who asks you to give an account for the hope that is in you, yet with gentleness and reverence" (1 Pet 3:15 NASB).

Pain (especially psychic or spiritual pain) *is* profane, and if your heartbroken friends are ever going to get beyond it, you'll have to let them label it any way they like. There's a similarity here between this process and the way many people face illness. Their first reaction is to ignore or deny it, as if by waiting the problem will resolve. Often, thankfully, this does happen.

But in terms of certain diseases, notably some cancers, denial can be deadly. The symptoms must be faced and once a person decides to do that, it doesn't make any sense or do any good to get into the examining room and act like nothing's wrong. Of course, most physicians will refuse to accept denial as truth, relentlessly probing your symptoms and history, searching for clues until both of you arrive at the only thing that will help – a label that describes your reality. Treating the symptoms might help, even without a label, but giving the problem a name is the only way really to pursue an effective treatment and cure.

In a similar way, pretending never helped a brokenhearted person become whole again. No responsible "soul doctor" will support that approach, since only telling the truth can begin the process of healing. But what if, in telling the truth, your brokenhearted friend insists on saying things that are irreverent or worse? Well then, rejoice – not in the impiety, but in the willingness to entrust the pain to you.

For instance, many Christians are angry at God for either

causing or allowing the event that has stolen their joy and broken their dreams. If your friend feels this way and trusts you enough, don't be surprised to hear, "I'm so mad I could spit. I thought God loved me, but not even somebody who hated me could hurt me more than this," and so on.

If you're ever privileged to hear honesty like this, you'll be as close to representing God as is humanly possible. So your response is extremely important, not only to your friend but also to God. In responding, remember Jesus who, as he hung on the Cross absorbing the hatred and abuse of those who put him there, said, "Father, forgive them; they don't know what they are doing."

You can bring this forgiveness into your friend's confusion by affirming those sentiments as legitimate expressions of their perspective at this point in time. For instance, you might say, "I've been disappointed sometimes, and even been angry with God for the way things have worked out. I worried about it at first, but then I realized my feelings couldn't possibly take God by surprise. Not only that, some people in the Bible like Moses got pretty upset with God at times, so I wasn't the first person, and you're not the last one, to feel that way toward God."

Expect One of Three Responses

If you'll do this sincerely, instead of trying to correct your friend's thinking, the response will likely take one of three directions. One might say, "Really? How did you get over it?" In this case, you could explain that when we have a problem with another person the best way to keep it from turning into bitterness that defiles and enslaves *us* is to confront, confess, forgive and be reconciled. Reconciling with God—the ultimate Person—means expressing the truth about how we feel and view things, including God's role, and choosing to lay aside the anger, resentment and bitterness so they will not further hinder our ability to love God. *When your friend is ready*, you might offer to be a witness to the prayer one will need to make in order to find release and reconciliation.

By contrast, your friend might say, "Maybe you worked it out, but I'm not interested. It's just totally, absolutely and eternally unfair. I don't care what you, God, or anybody in-between, tries to make me think or say!"

If this is the response, again rejoice, not because they insist on wallowing in their pain, but because they're willing to state their case without pretense. This gift of extreme vulnerability should be cherished and never treated with contempt by telling someone else what's been said.

In order to help such a friend, your biggest battle may not be with the friend—after all, you're trying to be an ally—but with *yourself*. The more you love your friend, the more the insistence on remaining in a prison of their own making will hurt *you*, because you long for them to find their way to freedom. Regardless of how strong your inclinations are to intervene, don't try to make them think or say *anything* at this point. They may be testing you to see whose agenda is really most important. They must discover if the love you represent (your own and God's) is real before their trust can be renewed.

If there's a principle involved, it's to consider doing the opposite of what your inclinations or religious training seems to suggest, because most of our common approaches are aimed at fulfilling *the helper's agenda* in one way or another. Stifle all your aspirations but one—to be an agent of grace in the midst of your friend's pain, patiently and prayerfully watching for the opportunity to introduce a flicker of hope into the dungeon of despair.

In *Pilgrim's Progress*, at one point Christian and his companion Hope are captured by Giant Despair and thrown into the dungeon of Doubting Castle. They languish there until Christian remembers, "What a fool I am to lie stinking in a dungeon when I may walk at liberty. I have a key in my bosom called Promise that I am persuaded will open any lock in Doubting Castle."[1]

Christian's key – Promise – was there all the time, but *he had to remember it was there*. This is the third possible response your friend could make and you can facilitate it by being the faithful companion in that cell.

When Giant Despair inquired why they should "choose to live when their lives were attended by such bitterness," Christian turned to Hope and said, "Brother, what shall we do? The life we now live is miserable. For my part, I do not know whether it is better to live this way or to die by our own hand. My soul chooses strangling rather than life, and the grave is easier for me than the dungeon. Shall we be ruled by the giant?"

Hope's answer is refreshing in its honesty: "Indeed, our present condition is dreadful, and death would be far more welcome than abiding this way forever ... [but] others have been taken by Giant Despair and have escaped. I am resolved to be patient and endure awhile and to try my utmost to get from under his hand."[2]

You don't have to force your friend to sing jolly tunes as you try to free yourselves from the dungeon of Doubting Castle. You just need to follow Hope's example: Validate reality, but encourage your friend to keep looking for a way out.

The Key Is a Person

God's *promises* unlock every door in the castle of Despair. And, as 2 Corinthians 1:20 makes clear, all God's promises are "Yes" in Christ. Jesus, the Promised One – whose life, death and resurrection point the way beyond even the most abject human pain – is the Divine antidote to brokenness, able to guard both heart and mind (see Phil 4:6-9).

How does he do it? First of all, he always tells the truth. And just as importantly, he speaks the truth in love.

As Jeremy reminded me, Jesus never forced his view of truth on anybody, because he "knew that a godly man or woman is *built*, line upon line, precept upon precept and that *only* the Holy Spirit can reveal God's truth to a person in a life-changing way, though seeds are often planted through the lives of others.

"Therefore," he added, "if I try to cram 'truth' down another person's throat to avoid personal suffering, I am only prolonging the process of growth and maturity in that person— the *opposite* of what is needed. This is why some people are never truly and completely healed. The Christian community around them isn't strong enough spiritually to endure with them long enough. Instead, most people end up trying to *act* healed in order to be accepted and loved."

In the previous chapter we looked at how Jesus might minister to the emotions of heartbreak. But how would he approach the mental confusion that also usually goes with it?

He would ask questions. For instance, he might ask:

- Can you change what's happened?
- Did you do everything you could?
- Are there others who need you?
- Do you really want to be healed?
- Can you still believe that God loves you?

He would tell a story. I created this fractured fairy tale not only to get a laugh, but to make a point:

Once upon a time there was a beautiful princess who lived with her father the king in their fairyland kingdom, where all was sweetness and light, and everyone lived happily ever after. Except for one thing. The princess was lonely, and often when she was lonely she would sit gazing into the reflecting pool by the side of the castle, wondering what would become of her and how she would ever meet the handsome prince of her dreams.

One day, while gazing into the pool, she noticed a frog sitting on a lily pad, a frog that seemed to be gazing at her, too. Now the princess was well versed in fairy tales, and she knew that sometimes evil spells were cast, turning handsome princes into frogs, and she began to think that perhaps this frog might be just such a prince in disguise.

Well, after many visits to the beautiful pool, and many encounters with this particular frog, the princess had finally made up her mind, and one day, she reached into the water, caught the frog and before she could change her mind, she kissed it, which she knew was the only way to liberate the prince from the spell.

Unfortunately for this particular princess, that kiss immediately transformed her into a frog and she spent the rest of her days serenading the palace guards.

Even fairy tales don't always come with happy endings. Life is full of unhappy surprises.

He would use symbols. Jeremy did this with one of his friends whose direction had become a serious concern. He sent him an old photo, and a little note: "Remember these two guys? They used to be real close." The message behind the message was: "I love you. I've been hanging onto you tooth and nail for a long time, man. But who are we really, now?"

He would use music. Although there's no biblical record of Jesus singing, I am confident, despite Barry Manilow's claims to the contrary, *Jesus* is music; he writes the songs—especially the songs that bridge the gap between the heart and mind. Sometimes music can find an entrance that plain words can't, and it speaks to the emotions and spirit as well as to the mind.

For Reflection or Discussion

1. If you have tried to work with alcoholics in the past, describe some of the difficulties, as well as some approaches that worked. If Billy were your friend, how would you have tried to intervene before he messed up the lives of so many other people?

2. Billy admitted he went on his last binge to test Shelly's limits. Do you think she was justified in kicking him out? What do you think of the timing (New Year's Day)? In a group setting, have two participants role-play the New Year's Day interchange between Shelly and Billy. Then debrief as a group and see if you can think of any way to rescue this marriage.

3. How did you react to the outburst, "If that's the way it's going to be, then God can go to h---!"
___ Honest, but extreme
___ Blasphemous
___ I wouldn't want my kids to read this
___ I wouldn't risk it, myself
___ Human, but not very spiritual
___ A key to his future healing
___ This question isn't fair

4. Suppose your friend has just said, "I'm so mad at God I could spit!" Can you see how hearing this kind of honesty is a privilege and "as close to representing God as is humanly possible"? How would you respond?

5. What does it mean to be "an agent of grace"?

6. Evaluate Jeremy's comments in relation to "lying about the truth." Is he right that there are too many that a church has not been able to reach because of a "propensity to turn our eyes away from the wound and pretend things are fine"? In a group setting, create and role-play a situation where this kind of denial is common.

7. Make up a fairy tale or story that summarizes your own journey with heartbreak. In a group setting, share it with the rest.

8. In a group setting, create a list of questions that might lead persons toward seeing the truth about the way they are handling heartbreak.

9. Discuss the role music can have – positive or negative – in helping people recover from loss. If a particular song has comforted you this way, share it in a group setting.

10. Read Philippians 4:6-9 and define the difference between the peace of God and the God of peace, and how knowing Jesus in a personal sense can introduce a peace that is able to guard both heart and mind. What is the key here, and how are both sides of this equation important in the journey of a heartbroken person toward wholeness?

10

Moving with the pain

Your friend may need a birthing coach

ANYBODY WHO COULD move away from a crowded, polluted, crime-infested metropolitan area to Colorado to work with a rapidly growing international Christian ministry with apparently limitless potential would be completely excited and eternally grateful. Right?

Not necessarily. At least not Esther, who had struggled all her life with feelings of deprivation and abandonment. Her parents loved each other so much that Esther (an only child) felt excluded. Some time after she married Bruce, who seemed so dependable, the problems they were facing got so overwhelming that he left, and she and the children never saw him again.

Esther buried herself in her work and kept a protective shield around her emotional self until many years later when she was able to live in the same home with her grandchildren for awhile. With them she developed a two-way love that was more free and secure and beautiful than anything she had ever experienced or imagined.

But then the company she worked for moved a thousand miles. Perhaps because she had a year's advance notice, the agony of leaving those little girls didn't really hit Esther until the weekend she moved into her new townhouse in Colorado. Suddenly all those old feelings of desertion, abandonment and fear let loose, far more intensely than she had expected.

"My first weekend here," she recalled, "was a three-day weekend which I spent crying at the top of my lungs and shaking my fist at God and saying, 'I can't do this. I can't live through this. Why should you make me do this? Why would you let this happen?'

"I wondered: *Is it ever going to stop? Is this ever going to get better? Who can I call that will tell me when it stops hurting? When do I stop feeling like I'm all raw and torn apart?*"

Several things aided Esther's recovery. The first was that God did not leave her alone in Colorado, but brought a new and very special friend into her life who understood her pain and was willing to walk through it with her.

But nearly as important was a choice Esther made about the way she would look at her situation. With time she realized that her anxieties were driven by the fear that God might leave her, too.

Insight, however, wasn't enough. It never is. In order for Esther to transform a heartbreaking change into an opportunity for growth, she had to make a conscious choice to view her situation differently. Instead of continuing to focus only on what she had left behind, she began looking for what she might gain by trusting God instead of questioning God.

"God showed me that God chose to make that separation so I could learn not to be dependent on anybody, or any situation, but only on God," Esther said. "I'm working toward that. It's not an easy thing. Sometimes I take two steps forward and three back—but overall I'm making progress. Little by little,

God is healing that fear of being alone and teaching me that Jim Elliot's perspective was right, 'You're never less alone than when you're alone with God.'

"So that's what I'm trying to learn during this time. I believe that eventually my son-in-law will find a job out here and we'll be close again," she added. "But I don't think it will happen until I'm dependent on God instead of the people in my life. The good thing about that is that when our family's together again, our relationships will be healthier, too."

Choices ... Changes

Many heartbroken people get stuck in a vain effort to change what has occurred so life can return to normal – the way things used to be. But no situation can ever be the way it used to be. As Heraclitus says, "You can't step in the same river twice." You'll get wet enough, but the water you stepped in before is now somewhere downstream.

When the loss comes through terminal illness, this struggle can be doubly difficult since the "good-bye" begins while the dying one is still alive and continues long after they're gone. To the grieving mind, it seems that anything other than clinging to what might have been seems disloyal to the deceased, especially if this was a child.

Frank, a pastor for many years, had numerous opportunities to help families change the way they were approaching crisis. The case that symbolized the rest was a four-year-old leukemia victim we'll call Jimmy.

Jimmy went through several remissions and relapses, an experience followed with deep concern by many church members. "We were on an emotional roller coaster for months," Frank recalled. "It was eating Jimmy's parents alive, along with his grandmother and some aunts and uncles who were part of the church.

"Toward the end, when Jimmy was failing, I went to call on the family. It was a long drive so all the way, I prayed:

Lord, give me wisdom. I don't know what to say, but I really want to help.

"When I got there, we passed the time of day for a little bit," Frank said, "and then I got serious with them and I said, 'I came with a very strange request tonight. I know that it's nothing you've ever heard before, but because I care, I want to help you. I've come tonight to ask you to give Jimmy to God.'

"You could have heard a pin drop for a long time. I didn't say anything; I just let them think about it awhile. Finally, I said, 'Through these years, we've prayed many times for Jimmy, and now it's apparent that probably God is not going to heal him. So I'd like for you to just place him in God's hands and trust God with the outcome. Do you think you could do that?' Jimmy's parents looked at each other and began to cry. Then his mother said, 'I could do that.' And his father said, 'I can, too.'

"So I prayed with them, and it was a pretty heavy evening. I tried to leave them on a positive note – that if they had committed Jimmy to God, then they could trust God with him. That was on Saturday. The following Tuesday night, late, I got a phone call that Jimmy was in the children's hospital in Denver; would I come?

"About midnight, it was obvious the boy wasn't going to make it. I'll never forget walking with that father to the end of the hall where there was a big window. He looked me straight in the eye and said, 'Pastor, I meant what I said Saturday night. I gave him to God. My commitment's still the same tonight; I just want you to know that.' I sensed that already he was beginning to heal. He already had something to lean on when Jimmy died.

"Then we went back into the room, and he put his arm around his wife and said the same thing to her, and she reaffirmed it. Within 45 minutes, their little boy was gone, but they were prepared and already beginning to work into their grief. It wasn't so much that I was with them – though I believe

God helped me help them. But what really helped them was that they consciously turned it over to God. Through this choice, they were saying, 'We're taking control of this situation by putting it in God's hands.'"

Facilitate Without Forcing

There are many paradoxes of faith, but this is one of the greatest – the way to gain control is by giving it to God. There are other similar paradoxes in the Scriptures, many of which relate to recovering from loss:

- We're wisest when we admit our foolishness.
- The way to gain real life is to lose our life in his.
- The way to wholeness is through being broken.
- We're strongest when we give our weakness to God.

Remember the apostle Paul's experience with his "thorn in the flesh"? God's message to him was "My grace is sufficient for you, for power is perfected in weakness." So, Paul says, "I am well content with weaknesses, with insults, with distresses, with persecutions, with difficulties, for Christ's sake; for when I am weak, then I am strong" (2 Co 12:9-10 NASB).

The paradoxes of God are enigmatic to the human mind, which wants to control, overcome and win. But God's consistent message (through both Old and New Testaments) is "the way to overcome is to give the control to me."

In the Garden of Gethsemane, the night he was betrayed Jesus agonized with his fate to the point of – according to Dr. Luke – sweating blood. "Father," Jesus prayed, "if thou art willing, remove this cup from me; yet not my will, but thine be done" (Lk 22:42 NASB).

When Jonathan became ill, I didn't know how to pray. I was too confused in heart and mind. Someone suggested that "Thy will be done" seemed rather passive in a situation like that. Through the lens of 25 years, however, those words have taken on increasing meaning and power.

To pray, "My will be done, regardless," is the epitome of un-faith. To pray, "Heal my son according to thy will" is the essence of trust, because it leaves the power where it really lies ... in the hands of God, which reduces our need to ensure any particular result. Don't misunderstand me. I would have died in Jonathan's place had God given me that choice. But the only choice I really had was whether or not I would embrace God's way with him rather than insisting on my own way.

Brokenhearted believers always face this choice—Will I hold on to the pain or consciously choose to give it all to God, by faith, trusting that:

- God knows what God is doing;
- God is motivated by love in everything God causes or allows;
- God really does understand the way I feel.

Long before his agony in the Garden, Jesus had "steadfastly set his face to go to Jerusalem," knowing full well what would happen there. Long before that choice, he chose to become a human being, to enter our pain for the purpose of redeeming it—and us—for the glory of God. Even before that, in the council of the Almighty, he had chosen to die, the "Lamb slain before the foundation of the world." In other words, before creating humankind, God already knew that by creating us with freedom to choose, God was writing God's own death sentence.

So God knows about heartbreak, from the pain of creating beings God knew would reject God, to the grief of watching God's own Son die. As the Suffering Servant:

> He was despised and forsaken of men,
> A man of sorrows, and acquainted with grief,...
> Surely our griefs He Himself bore,
> And our sorrows He carried;...
> He was pierced through for our transgressions,
> He was crushed for our iniquities;
> The chastening for our well-being fell upon Him,
> And by his scourging we are healed (Is 53:3-5 NASB).

Jesus fully entered our reality, becoming our great High Priest who understands our weaknesses because he was "tempted in all things as we are, yet without sin. Let us therefore draw near with confidence to the throne of grace, that we may receive mercy and may find grace to help in time of need" (from Heb 4:15-16 NASB).

God hurts when we hurt. When you ache with your broken-hearted friend, you emulate the *heart* of God. When you long to communicate truth to your friend as an anchor for their soul, you emulate the *mind* of God. But when you help a friend choose to work with God to redeem the pain for God's glory, only the *method* of God can produce the desired result. God never forces anyone to trust God. It is God's *kindness*, not God's power or even God's persuasiveness, that leads to repentance.

If God will never force your heartbroken friends to embrace God's way, you must resist any tendency to push for resolution. As long as you force, most will resist. But if you love God enough, you'll entrust the outcome to God. And *if you love your friends enough*, you'll set them free to choose.

There's a risk involved—they may choose contrary to what you know is best for them. They may turn away from faith. They may even turn away from you. But if this happens, you'll have an opportunity to understand the heartbreak of God when the race created in God's own image chose against God (and continues to do so).

Discernment, wisdom, timing, sensitivity and faith are essential here, perhaps more than at any other point in your journey with friends through heartbreak toward wholeness. And prayer is key to all of them, because what's really happening is spiritual in nature—a warfare for a friend's soul—where the outcome is in doubt until they decide which way they will move with the pain.

Your role will be like that of a birth coach whose function is to help a woman in labor use the pain properly, in a process that leads through agony to joy. Sometimes the coach says "pant and blow" to counteract the contractions, because pushing too early would only hurt the baby as well as the mother. Between contractions, the coach may offer some ice chips and a cool, damp towel to wipe the woman's brow. But the coach's crucial role is supportive—another person willing to share the mother's pain—until the marvelous moment when it's time to push that baby into the hands of the waiting doctor or midwife.

If you've ever given birth with the help of a coach, you'll understand immediately the value of having that objective person involved. Your heartbroken friend has a similar need, since there are times when the pain is so great and the experience so exhausting it is nearly impossible to gain a realistic perspective on what's happening.

Coffin or Cocoon

Some time ago I saw an interview with a mother whose nine-year-old daughter's murder was still unsolved. Even eight months after the funeral, the mother hadn't changed the girl's room. She made it clear that she would *never* change it. But she may.

Grief like this can be either a coffin or a cocoon. If it's a coffin, the epitaph will read: Died at 30, buried at 70. If it's a cocoon, someday a new creation will emerge, far more beautiful than any broken person dreamed of becoming.

Every heartbroken person faces this predicament: Which will it be—coffin or cocoon? Both are painful, involving a "death" of sorts. The former is easier, since its primary focus is the past. Hurtful as the experience may have been, it is still more comfortable to cling to the known than to launch into the unknown. But choosing to spin the cocoon is far more constructive, despite its risks. Flying gracefully through the air is always better than rotting from the inside out.

Metamorphosis is where God is going in your friend's life, but you can't force them to coöperate. You can only help them choose. Here are some suggestions:

- Ask them to identify their most important issues. Once the list exists, ask them to choose one they want to do something about and then work with them on this one thing until it is resolved. Then go on to the next one *they want to tackle*. Hint: Don't force them to prioritize the list and work on the hardest things first. Baby steps forward are better than regression.

- Help the friend focus on positive things, at least once a day, by sending cards, leaving notes, calling, or in many other creative ways. You're helping them fulfill Philippians 4:8: "Whatever is true ... honorable ... right ... pure ... lovely ... of good repute, if there is any excellence and if anything worthy of praise, let your mind dwell on these things" (NASB). The ultimate healing focus for the mind is in worship and praise—so when they're ready you might invite them along with you to church. Even before that, you could provide musical tapes and other uplifting materials.

- Look for and discuss situations in the news (or some other neutral setting) like the mother who refused to change her murdered daughter's room. For instance, you might comment, "She must have really loved her daughter. Can a person ever recover from something like that?" This could lead—but don't force it—to the importance of choices, perspectives and other issues mentioned in this chapter. If it does, you might ask: "Where do you want to be in five years—or three years, or even next year?" Or when they're ready, ask, "What do you think God wants (or expects) of you after this experience?"

- Remember—and communicate to the friend—that metamorphosis is gradual, not an instantaneous change. Accepting this will impact your patience quotient—as well as your friend's own expectations.

Nancy Miller was working as an interpreter at a Mennonite hospital in Haiti when her three-day-old son died. She wrote, "I had a real tough time because I had no one who had experienced the death of a child. I felt I should be finished with my grieving after a week."

Instead of seven days, however, Nancy's grieving lasted seven *years*, until she finally faced her anger at God. Thankfully, having resolved it, she has been able to use the experience to minister to others. "I was trying to help a mother who had a handicapped child," she wrote. "I asked her if she might be angry with God. She replied, 'No, you can't get angry with God.' I helped her see God was very capable of handling our anger and she said, 'Yes, I am angry at God. My father was an alcoholic, my mother is in a mental institution and now I have a handicapped child.' We worked through the anger process and she became a different mother. A couple of weeks later I heard her ask another mother, 'Are you angry at God? You know you can be – God can handle your anger. Mrs. Miller was, and she's a Mennonite!'"

Share stories like this one with your friend, using them to hasten the move beyond their anger toward the reconciliations that must take place – with God, others and themselves – in order to become whole. As someone moves in that direction, they will be participating in what Peter Kreeft calls "spiritual judo" – using the enemy's force against him.

This has happened for Theresa, who described her life as one "filled with overwhelming amounts and types of pain ... child abuse/molestation, never-ending ridicule, the loss of many friends (I couldn't change my outlook on life according to *their* timetable), the deaths of both of my parents and two very special aunts (all within a two-year period), physical disability in both legs, then a back injury which has caused pain beyond description, lung disorders, clinical depression, and more."

But Theresa adds, "Physically, I hurt, but spiritually, I'm becoming stronger in faith, increasing in hope, and developing my love for others. Currently, my ministry includes face painting for children during outreach programs, learning guitar and singing. I love the Lord and am *really* learning that God loves me, too!"

For Reflection or Discussion

1. How would you have tried to help Esther during her first long weekend of separation from her family which she spent crying at the top of her lungs and shaking her fist at God:

__ By saying, "Get a grip on it, Esther. My goodness, you're a grown woman."

__ By sitting with her and trying to understand her pain.

__ By inviting her out to a local comedy club.

__ By calling all her friends and asking them to pray for her.

__ By having her over to your house for a quiet dinner.

__ By leaving her alone so she could get it out in privacy.

__ Other:

2. In Esther's case, insight was important in motivating her choice of how to approach this brokenness. Put into your own words what insight you think helped her most and recall (and share, if you wish, in a group setting) any similar experiences you have had.

3. Evaluate Pastor Frank's approach to Jimmy's parents. How did you respond when you read his words, "I've come tonight to ask you to give Jimmy to God"?

__ He was misinformed about God's promise to heal.

__ He was just trying to get it off his own mind.

__ His guidance helped them to be more realistic.

__ His involvement showed them the path toward their own healing.

__ It was just a mind game in the end. What difference did it really make?

__ Other:

4. Discuss the "paradoxes of faith" concept, and make a list of any biblical teachings or examples that support the idea that the ways of God are often the opposite of what human beings would choose. To get you started, here are a few, some of them mentioned in the text:

__ The way to gain control is to give it to God.
__ We're strongest when we give our weakness to God.
__ We're wisest when we admit our foolishness.
__ We're richest when we've become poor for God's sake.
__ The way to be exalted is to humble yourself.
__ The way to gain life is to lose it.
__ The way to be first is to be last.
__ The way to gain authority is to become a servant.

[Author's note: If you (or your group) develop an expanded list, please send it to me: dbbv1@aol.com.]

5. Is praying "Not my will, but thine be done" a passive approach or a difficult, conscious choice? Is there any difference between this prayer and "Heal our son, according to Thy will"? Share experiences you have had with this.

6. Which of these assertions is the hardest to accept in the face of a devastating experience?

- God knows what God is doing;
- God is motivated by love in everything God causes or allows;
- God really does understand the way I feel.

7. Support (or challenge) the idea that God hurts when we hurt. If you think it is true, how might believing this be helpful to a brokenhearted person?

8. How does the knowledge that Jesus "was tempted in all things as we are, yet without sin" increase your confidence in coming to the throne of grace in time of need?

__ It doesn't, since he never sinned.
__ Not too much, but I do it anyway.
__ Quite a lot, because mercy is most valuable from one who has walked in shoes a lot like mine.
__ Maximally, because while someone who had succumbed to temptation might be able to sympathize with me, "grace to help" can really only come from One who never gave in.

9. Why is granting someone the freedom of choice so crucial in terms of eventual recovery?

10. In a group setting, discuss the analogy of becoming your heartbroken friend's "birth coach" in terms of both methods and goals. List as many similarities as you can. How do these compare to the way God "labors" with us?

11. Imagine that the bereaved mother whose nine-year-old daughter's murder is still unsolved is your good friend. It's now been two years since the funeral, but she still refuses to change the girl's room. How would you try to help this woman? What choices does she need to make in order to get past the stage she's in? Is her grief at this point a coffin or a cocoon?

12. It took Nancy seven *years* to realize and resolve her anger with God for allowing her three-day-old baby to die. Based on your own experience with loss (or trying to help someone else work through theirs), what do you think of this example?

__ Rare—perhaps the circumstances made it worse.

__ Uncommon—but some people do become angry with God.

__ Typical—at least in people of her religious heritage.

__ Common—most people get angry with God, but repress it.

__ Exemplary—everyone should approach it this way.

__ Other:

11

Beauty for ashes

The deeper the hurt, the more meaningful the healing.

DEAR GOD,

Do you really cause or allow everything to happen? Sometimes you do something special (like a miracle) for someone. How do you choose who to do that for?

Just what value does prayer have anyway? And what value is there in trying to raise these children for you? We tried, trusted and prayed. *This* is your answer?

After all that happened to Job, couldn't you have said something to him that showed that you understood? Were his children pawns in your test? How could you do that to your faithful servant? Job was one man, one real live hurting person—all that tremendous pain for a lesson to the rest of the world? You allowed (or even caused—you brought Job's name up) all that pain and we are supposed to recognize that you love Job?

It is so difficult to interpret your Word. How do we ever really know just what you mean?

I expected you to hold me. *Where are you?*

Is Angie okay?

—Jenny (do you know who I am?)

Jenny's letter to God was her answer to the last question of the survey I used to gather insights for this book: "In terms of your own lingering issues with this loss, what question(s) keep coming back into your mind that you might like to ask God?"

After Jenny's daughter Angie died of a self-inflicted, apparently accidental gunshot wound (see chapter 5), for a long time Jenny had more questions than answers. But her church friends didn't want Jenny's doubt to hang out: "I was absolutely desperate for people," she wrote. "I needed mature Christians who were able and willing to deal with the issue of pain to let me question God. I tried bringing up God issues with Christians I respected, but they simply could/would not deal with it. We must teach our churches to allow people to question God. The statement in your book [*If God Is So Good, Why Do I Hurt So Bad?*] to 'not fake it or even you'll not know when it's real' has helped a lot. If I ever worship God again, it will be with *all* of me."

The Heart of the Matter

The last barrier to recovery is spiritual. The last frontier your heartbroken friend must cross in the journey toward wholeness requires reconciliation with a God who claims to love everyone but has allowed at least this Christian to experience heartbreak. Based on years of listening, I believe that one of the most common – though not always verbalized – questions is: *Where were you, God, when I needed you?*

The feelings of abandonment, even betrayal, are often most intense for those who loved God intensely before their loss occurred. So don't be surprised, and don't despair, if your formerly very orthodox friends seem to lose their spiritual bearings for awhile.

Your assignment, if you choose to accept it, is to stick as close to them as you possibly can, because their adversary (and yours) is deceitful, crafty and very experienced in turning perplexity into doubt and distrust into deep spiritual despondency. The evil one's goal is, was, and always will be to destroy all evidence in our world that God is alive, active and able to redeem even the most painful experiences for God's good purposes.

The stakes are high—even beyond your friend's personal wholeness. For God's method of presenting evidence of God's redemptive presence to a skeptical world is, was, and always will be through redeemed people like us. Our mission—should we choose to accept it—is to develop deeper faith, for if we do, we and our friend will be able to connect with the broken world far better than a thousand three-point sermons ever will.

The good news in your friend's journey toward resolution is: *The deeper the hurt, the more meaningful the healing can be.* As I've written elsewhere, the capacity for pain is an indicator of one's potential for joy. Or, to paraphrase Job's conclusion: "I thought I knew you, God. But that former knowledge was like *hearing about you* versus actually *knowing you personally.*"

The only way to get from hearsay faith to eyewitness faith is by asking questions like those that Job—and Jenny—asked. The harder the better. The questioner's level of openness with God is evidence, not of insolence or heresy, but of relationship. Otherwise, why bother?

Hard Questions

Most heartbroken believers have questions they'd like to ask God:

- "I would like to ask God what role God played in ending a beautiful, green-eyed teenager's life," Loretta wrote, after her 17-year-old son survived four major surgeries following a motorcycle accident only to die from an undetected blood clot. "I find that after almost nine years, I am *less* able to talk about it. It really depresses me."
- "In Matthew 7:9 you asked, 'Which of you, if a child asks for bread, will give them a stone?'" wrote Sandra, a victim of childhood abuse followed by multiple sclerosis as an adult. "You implied no father would do that—but that's the kind of father I had. I wish you had talked more about *him* and what

to do, how to become whole after having an unkind father. It would have made it so much more possible to trust you.

"Also – what do you want me to *do* in this altered body? Did you cause this to happen to me? If so, what for? If you'd just clue me in, I'd go along. Otherwise, it seems like such a waste and you seem like just another cruel father. Where is the love you promised?"

- "God, how can you take a mom's greatest fear, the death of her child, and mend her heart, allow her to smile again (or) believe you that good things might come out of such a tragedy? How do you do it?" asked Wendy, whose 20-year-old son was struck and killed by an automobile.

Understanding Your Role

If your friend entrusts these hardest questions to you, your first instinct may be to reach for a concordance – or even a multi-volume set of systematic theology – to find a "truth-byte" addressing each concern. But to save you a lot of time and agonizing, here's a little secret: *Your friend is not as interested in hearing answers to the questions as you are in providing them.*

You could verify it easily enough by asking: "If I could find the perfect answer to every question you've raised, would you be satisfied?"

Warning: Don't ask this unless *you know for sure* the heartbroken persons wants to face the real issues driving the questions. This is very hard to discern. Even when people seem ready, they rarely are. And many cannot handle the idea that they would rather take you in circles than deal with what's really bugging them.

Sometimes people do this when we try to witness to them. The intellectual types, especially, can keep you running for weeks in an effort to refute each of the many supposedly sincere objections. But you can discover spiritual sincerity by asking, "If I could prove to you beyond any reasonable doubt that Jesus is the risen Son of God, would you accept him?"

If they are as sincere as they want you to believe, the answer will be: "Yes, I would," or "I don't know." But only the truly honest will admit, "No, I don't think so." Many times, the real issue blocking a decision to accept Christ is the person's unwillingness to exchange the life they now have for the one God desires for them in Christ.

The core issue for your brokenhearted friend may be similar: *Am I or am I not willing to exchange my brokenness for the ministry God has designed for me?*

No one can make such decisions for another person, and forcing capitulation will only hinder progress toward resolution. So, if your friends aren't ready yet to pursue the exchange in question, don't chastise them for refusing to surrender to God. That's really a highly personal matter between them and God.

Instead, stop and ask the Lord to clarify *what God wants your role to be* – sounding board, encourager, debater, exhorter, what? Very likely, God wants you to be a minister of reconciliation, an ambassador for Christ, appealing to your friend: "I beg you, on Christ's behalf, be reconciled to God." The original words in 2 Corinthians 5:20 are "as though God were *calling* [appealing] through us." *Calling* is from the word used to describe the role of the Holy Spirit [*parakaleo*], the One *called alongside*. Your primary role, as one called alongside your friend, is *diplomatic*. Your mission is to be God's agent of redemption in your friend's life.

You can't do this in the ultimate sense that only Jesus could accomplish in terms of salvation as our redeemer. But there is a sense in which "redeem" can be applied to recovery from heartbreak. In the midst of one of the most practical discussions of Christian living in the New Testament, Paul says, "Be very careful [literally: *see carefully*], then, how you live [literally: *walk*] – not as unwise but as wise, making the most of every opportunity [literally: *redeeming the time*], because the days are evil. Therefore do not be foolish, but understand what the Lord's will is" (Eph 5:15-17).

Depending on what stage they're at in processing their pain, your friends may be either care*ful* or care*less* about how they're living, specifically which way they're walking in relation to God –

toward God or away. But if they're ever going to get beyond their pain, they must come to see their experience wisely, as an opportunity to counteract the fact that the days are evil because the evil one is bent on destroying their faith and their witness.

But there is more to it – as Job's story clearly demonstrates. God, who could have prevented your friend's pain, allowed it because God could foresee how their brokenness would produce the kind of strength, character and true spirituality that they earnestly desire. This, too, is a paradox of faith; and embracing God's way with us – especially when it involves being broken so we can be made whole according to God's design – is one of the hardest choices a heartbroken believer will ever make. Our privilege as helpers is to facilitate and not hinder this choice.

For Reflection or Discussion

1. Why might Jenny's friends have been reluctant to have her bring up "the God issues"?

2. List any "God issues" you have had over the years, and discuss how open you thought your Christian friends were to hearing you out.

3. Evaluate Jenny's statement, "If I ever worship God again, it will be with *all* of me":

__ As long as she says "if," her attitude is wrong.

__ The fact she can even think of worshiping again is positive.

__ I don't know if *I've* ever worshiped God with all of me.

__ God would be satisfied with any part of her she can offer.

__ With God, it's all or nothing.

__ Other:

4. Why might a person's sense of betrayal by God be greater if their previous love for God was intense?

5. How might the degree of alienation expressed be an indicator of something hopeful?

6. Which of the "hard questions" most fully connected with you? If you were that person's friend, how would you RESPOND?

7. In a group setting, choose one of the cases and role-play a conversation between that person and a best friend, making sure to include these two components: 1) The hurting person is not as interested in hearing answers to questions as the friend is in providing them; 2) Because of this, the helper becomes exasperated enough to ask: "If I could find the perfect answer to every question you've raised, would you be satisfied?"

Debrief, listing any positive or negative principles of helping that can be derived from the role play. After focusing only on that interchange, add any other principles that come to mind from the chapter or from your own experience.

8. If your main role is to be Christ's ambassador to your heartbroken friend, what message have you been asked to deliver? How does your role impact your methods, choice of words, responses, etc.? Use 2 Corinthians 5:11-6:1 to guide your discussion in a group setting.

9. List the parallel issues in:

Exchanging your unregenerate life for the one God has called you to in Christ....	Exchanging your brokenness for the ministry God has designated for you...
_____	_____
_____	_____
_____	_____
_____	_____
_____	_____

In a group setting—
     Discuss any surprises when you combine your lists.
     What is the issue most often involved?
     How can you help a broken person resolve this issue?

10. Is it proper to think of yourself as God's agent of redemption as you help your friend recover?

__ Of course not, only Jesus is the Redeemer
__ Rather egotistical
__ It's their problem; they have to save themselves from it
__ A good goal, but an awesome responsibility
__ Is this another trick question?

11. If it weren't for a sense of God's calling on your life, where would you be? What value has there been in pursuing God's way rather than your own?

12. Use this space to write a thank-you note to God for this expression of God's grace:

Seven habits of highly effective comforters

Become a pathfinder through the wilderness of heartbreak

NEXT TO THE Bible, the book that has most impacted my thinking is *The 7 Habits of Highly Effective People* by Stephen R. Covey, which describes a multi-faceted model for creating the most effective personal and corporate relationships.

With a tip of the hat to Dr. Covey – and apologies for the comparative superficiality of what I'm about to do with some of his concepts – I want to take one more look at our subject with a view toward what can happen *in you* as you try to help your heartbroken friend.

Habit #1: Be Proactive

When you first discover your friend is facing something devastating, take the initiative *to go to help* rather than waiting for a call or some other signal of need. One of the questions on my survey was: "Based on your experience, how do you try to help someone you know is brokenhearted?" A common theme was: "Be there, be there, be there."

There is no substitute. A phone call or letter or especially a telegram will communicate your concern, but in retrospect what your friend will remember is who came – who stayed – who cared enough to meet them, person to person, and actually share their pain when the crisis was the most intense.

You don't have to say much. A hug, some tears and a few words can communicate volumes. After the diagnosis of my second son's illness, my brother Paul came over immediately. When I opened the door, he said more *in two words* than some people said during the whole ordeal. "Oh, Dave," he said, as he reached out to embrace me. All we had to do was look into each other's eyes, share the hurt and be thankful we had each other.

People in crisis will normally be reluctant to ask *anyone* to come, unless they become totally desperate (or know for sure the person in question will *lighten their load*). This is not antisocial. Because what's going on already has drained their energy and threatens their equilibrium, they can't deal with another obligation (beyond survival), including having to explain, converse or in some other way *give* to whoever shows up. So only rarely will heartbroken people call for help, even when many people have said, "Call if you need anything."

However, if you ever do get a call, consider it an S.O.S. Drop everything and get there fast. The only stops you should make are at an ATM to get some cash to put in the homemade card you're going to leave with your friend, and a pizza place, sub shop or donut stand – depending on the hour and your friend's favorite food.

On your way, pray. That's as spiritually proactive as you get. Become your friend's advocate before the throne of grace. When you get there, communicate this message: *We're in this together. We may not be able to control the situation or change what's taken place, but together we will find a way through it.*

Now, about that card. No pretty store-bought card can accomplish what your own words can if you ask the Spirit of

God for a creative way to express the love you feel. So what I'm suggesting you do is make a word-gift to leave with your friend.

What to say? Here are several examples from a group to which I once belonged. The participants were asked to bring a word gift for the person whose name they had drawn the previous week. Here are some examples, each reflecting needs the recipient had expressed at some time during the course of the group's existence:

- "My gift to you would be an internal hug you would feel continuously. It would be a sense of security and warmth, that would make you feel competent and loved."
- "I would give you everything the locusts have eaten plus a double measure of God's Spirit to enable you to minister God's healing to other pilgrims."
- "Complete joy. God's deep, satisfying joy. Joy in living, joy in loving, joy in giving, joy in being. Then, joy in seeing your dreams come true."

You don't have to be a poet or writer to give your friend a gift like this, since "A word aptly spoken is like apples of gold in settings of silver" (Prov 25:11). The main prerequisite is envisioning how they are feeling at this moment and then trying to fill that hole with your love. If you will engage in proactive inventiveness like this, you have already begun to fulfill the next habit.

Habit #2: Begin with the End in Mind

If you could project yourself to the end of the next twelve months, what would you need to see in your friend's journey through heartbreak in order for you to feel you had been a successful helper? Secondarily, what would you need to see within yourself as a result of your journey with them in order for you to feel the Lord had accomplished all God had in mind *for you* in this experience?

The most effective helpers have a clear sense of mission, whether it be what they are trying to accomplish or what God would like to accomplish through them. This is a difficult though not impossible assignment in relation to something as personal as heartbreak, because it's tempting to approach it in terms of helping people think, speak or act in some theologically correct manner. *But the core issue of recovery has to do with being, not doing.* With that in mind, just for a moment, pause, close your eyes and imagine a conversation between yourself and this friend a year from now:

Where are you? Is it day or night, outdoors or indoors, in a public place or a quiet hideaway? What are you talking about? What kind of words are being used–especially their emotional content? Do you feel free, driven or constrained in some way? Is your friend at peace, anxious, upset or angry? Are you better friends in this future interchange than you are today? How are you both different from the way you used to be?

Now, how do you plan to get from where you are right now–say, preparing to go to the hospital to be at the bedside of the mother who has just had a heart attack and is not expected to live through the night–to where you would like to help them be a year from now?

Of course, I hope you'll keep in mind all the things we've talked about in this book, including being sensitive and patient with them through the first few months. But at some point, they'll be ready to move ahead because they don't want to stay where they are any more. Will you be ready to help the friend capitalize on this change and help them move in a constructive direction?

Some other friends may push them–at least that's the way it will feel to them. But for every push, there's at least an unconscious resistance, because we don't really know if we can, or should, implicitly trust people who try to force us in *any direction*, regardless of how wholesome and good it may appear to be, to them or to us.

The reason you'll be able to help is because you've been walking beside them, listening, sharing and caring. But at some point it will be time to lead. The key question, therefore, is, "Do you know where you're going?" This is where the visualization we started this section with comes in. For Christian helpers, the underlying issue is, "Where is God going in my friend's life (and in our experience together)?"

For each person you try to help, the answer will be unique, but the main objective will be the same. Where God is going in every believer's life is found in Romans 8:28-29: "And we know that God causes all things to work together for good to those who love God, to those who are called according to his purpose. For whom he foreknew, he also predestined to become conformed to the image of his Son, that he might be the first-born among many brethren ..." (NASB).

If you both love God, then you *both* are "called according to God's purpose." This means you have a calling or mission. The way out of heartbreak's wilderness starts at the point where this truth is internalized, becoming the central guiding principle around which all else can be arranged. God is able—because God is greater—to cause *anything* to work for good, regardless of how it feels to us at any given moment. Will you dedicate yourself to helping your friend choose to coöperate with God toward that end? The answer will depend on just how focused you can become (and remain) on the most important things.

Habit #3: Put First Things First

In the Christian life in general, people fail to accomplish all they could for God not only because they don't know what they're trying to accomplish, but because they allow the good to distract them from the better and the better to deter them from the best.

You don't necessarily have to like climbing down in that pit with Charlie (remember chapter 5). The decisive factor is that your purpose to help him out of that pit is given precedence over the degree of your dislike for the way Charlie's problems put a damper on your personal enjoyment of life. In other words, for the joy set before you—his wholeness—you have laid aside certain of your rights to become his servant in the process, regardless of how long it takes. As a friend of mine used to say, "A servant is a person who delights in making another person successful."

Earlier in this chapter, I asked you to envision what your friend's successful recovery would look like. Now, as you think about helping "Charlie" move toward that goal, the question has become: *What one thing could you do this week (or month) with Charlie that would most likely have a long-term positive impact on his recovery?*

Instead of focusing on Charlie's problems—although you may need to let him keep telling you about them until he tires of hearing his own repetition—focus instead on that one thing and how you can facilitate its occurrence. If you don't, Charlie's problems could lead you both down a bunch of fruitless rabbit trails, and a year from now you'll be right where you are, wondering why.

To help you get started, let's think about what *category* of progress would be most helpful to your heartbroken friend. The best answer, I predict, lies in any direction that would increase their ability to help themselves. Ultimately you are not striving for a dependent relationship, but interdependence. When this is over, you want to be functioning side by side in the body of Christ, each fulfilling the role God chose for you long before the loss that brought you together in your present mutually therapeutic relationship.

As you lead your friend in that direction, there will be times when you must say no to some things in order to say yes to others. For instance, in order to maintain your identity while encouraging your friend to take responsibility for their problems, you may have to fight their attempts to draw you in, even absorb you, in issues that are totally their own.

The most significant example of this is the relationship with God, where at the very core of things nobody else can be either a buffer or a scapegoat. The friend may have to wrestle it out, like Jacob and the angel and as an observer you may have to fight your inclination to intervene, protect or even referee.

But the ultimate reason you'll stay out of it is because when you put first things first, your friend's need for reconciliation with God takes precedence over your fear of a turn away from God, instead. (If that happens, you can still walk beside them until they're ready to turn back.)

To take this a step further, your friend's need for reconciliation with God is really the number one priority of your journey together through heartbreak and beyond, because until you both have come to that place, *nothing else will ever really fit or put the pieces of life back together.* As long as at the center there is alienation, fragmentation or destructive energy of any sort, any recovery will be only partial and temporary.

A few years ago, J. Grant Howard published an insightful and challenging book, *Balancing Life's Demands*, in which he demonstrated that the priority system frequently used by modern Christians is not aligned with what Jesus said. You've heard the list: God, family, church, work, witness and finally yourself. By contrast, Jesus said that the whole of divine revelation before his coming could be summarized in the commands to love God with all your heart, soul, mind and strength and your neighbor as yourself. Dr. Howard proposed another model with God at the center and everything else related to God, like parts of a wheel. In other words, the question of priorities is really a question of relationships and responsibilities that all connect at the center with God.

Therefore, if you want to help heartbroken friends reorganize their life, the primary question becomes not what's first, second or third, but how does their core relationship with God impact all their other concerns? In order to get them to see this, you're going to have to show them how you've worked this out (or are working it out) yourself. To the degree you succeed, you will create a situation where you both can win.

Habit #4: Think Win/Win

One of the biggest problems with Christian helpers is that their help comes with strings attached – usually the person's alignment with a particular viewpoint or dogma. This less-than-subtle message has more to do with conformity than with mutual discovery of what God is trying to teach both helper and friend through the experience.

Anyone who pressures a hurting friend in this way is repeating the error of Job's comforters, who tried to force Job's grief through the matrix of "good things happen to good people." Today's theologies are more sophisticated but no less coercive. As one of my respondents pointed out, God is not religious. God's viewpoint is so far above and beyond anybody's system that we do God a grave injustice when we force God, or *people who are trying to find God* – precisely your friend's problem – through any religion's grid. The only way to a therapeutic relationship where both can benefit, therefore, is to agree with C.S. Lewis's analysis in *The Chronicles of Narnia*, "Aslan [Jesus] is not a tame lion."

If you want to approach helping by asking, "How can we both win?" you must lay aside any agenda that might prevent you and your heartbroken friend from gaining significantly from the journey you've undertaken together. You need to communicate: *I'm not the expert here to give you the goods, nor do you have to capitulate to anybody's party line. I'm just another pilgrim in a process of discovery about who God is and how God is working in our world today, specifically, in and through the painful experience that has brought us together.*

Your heartbroken friend will never fully trust you as long as you have any other agenda in mind except their wholeness before God. In order to prove worthy of this trust, you may have to protect your friend from all assaults on their integrity by the religious among us who offer affirmation in return for spouting "the party line."

Win/win lies in another direction, in giving yourself completely to your friend, regardless of what their response may be. Dr. Covey quotes Dag Hammarskjöld, late secretary-general of the United Nations: "It is more noble to give yourself completely for one individual than to labor diligently for the salvation of the masses."[1]

If you will consciously choose (every time a choice is necessary) *for your friend and against the masses*, you may become the target of some pious person's reproach. But you and your friend will both win in the end, because what will happen as you walk together is that both of you will begin to see each new challenge, whether from without or within, as an opportunity in disguise. This is what seeing life with the eyes of faith is all about. But it can only happen if your eyes are open, not shut, to the hidden benefits of facing adversity.

Remember the situation in the Old Testament when Elisha and Gehazi, his servant, were surrounded by the enemy and Gehazi said, "Oh, my lord, what shall we do?" Elisha's response was to offer encouragement: "Don't be afraid.... Those who are with us are more than those who are with them." Then the prophet prayed, "O LORD, open his eyes so he may see." When Gehazi took another look at the enormous problem, he saw instead that the hills were "full of horses and chariots of fire all around Elisha" (see 2 Ki 6:15-17).

If you stick with your friend faithfully enough, you may be privileged to have the role of Elisha. But in order to fulfill it, you will have to listen to their concerns and try to understand and share them, before offering *any* solution, spiritual or otherwise. Following the prophet's example, don't chastise your friend for having less than adequate faith, but try to understand their concern, encourage them and then pray that God would help them comprehend the realities of the situation you're both

How to Help a Heartbroken Friend

trying to see more clearly.

Habit #5: Seek First to Understand, Then to Be Understood

In general, helpers spend far too much time talking and not enough listening. Their help, therefore, is often irrelevant because it fails to connect with the friend's real need. There is simply no way around finding the open door of need and entering your friend's brokenness through that avenue, as opposed to "dealing with it" in some prepackaged format.

Dr. Covey opens his chapter on this habit with an illustration that provides an excellent transition between Gehazi's problem and God's solution (my application, not Covey's):

> Suppose you've been having trouble with your eyes and you decide to go to an optometrist for help. After briefly listening to your complaint, he takes off his glasses and hands them to you. "Put these on," he says. "I've worn this pair of glasses for ten years now and they've really helped me. I have an extra pair at home; you can wear these."
>
> So you put them on, but it only makes the problem worse. "This is terrible!" you exclaim. "I can't see a thing!"
>
> "Well, what's wrong?" he asks. "They work great for me. Try harder."
>
> "I am trying," you insist. "Everything is a blur."
>
> "Well, what's the matter with you? Think positively."
>
> "Okay. I positively can't see a thing."
>
> "Boy, are you ungrateful!" he chides. "And after all I've done to help you!"[2]

You wouldn't bother to go back to a doctor like that, yet this is exactly the treatment your heartbroken friend has received from many people who have tried to help: Without any diagnostic workup, your friend has been handed glasses that work for somebody else. Depending on the group of people involved, those glasses may work for *everybody* else. Nevertheless, they *don't* (and really *can't*) work for the one who is having trouble trying to see what God is doing or where God is going in their life.

In Gehazi's case, although Elisha wanted his servant to see

with spiritual eyes, even the great prophet couldn't make it happen. All he could do was pray, because it was really up to God to correct Gehazi's visual acuity. Once that happened, Gehazi saw the horses and chariots of fire. Interestingly, it does not say Gehazi saw exactly the same thing as Elisha, who perhaps even saw the warriors in the chariots.

No two people can have the same vision of spiritual realities, after all. There will be similarities – search the Scriptures for yourself sometime, comparing the visions God gave to the prophets. In fact, there *must be* differences in both content and meaning in each case, because the communication of God as interpreted by the Holy Spirit to the heart and mind of each believer is uniquely suited to that person's position on the journey of faith.

So, you need to find ways to keep asking your friend what God is showing or telling them, or what God has been teaching. There are as many ways to do this as there are people, but you must avoid one thing – asking rhetorical questions whose sole purpose is to provide an opportunity for you to make your own point. Your integrity as a friend is at stake in the way you handle this. To the degree that you help your friend share what God has been communicating, you will progress together toward the next step, communion (or in Covey's terminology: synergy).

Habit #6: Synergize

"Simply defined, it [synergy] means that the whole is greater than the sum of its parts," Dr. Covey states. "It means that the relationship which the parts have to each other is a part in and of itself. It is not only a part, but the most catalytic, the most empowering, the most unifying, and the most exciting part."

He goes on to describe the creative process involved in this as "terrifying ... because you don't know exactly what's going to happen or where it is going to lead. You don't know what new dangers and challenges you'll find.

"Without doubt," he adds, "you have to leave the comfort zone of base camp and confront an entirely new and unknown wilderness. You become a trailblazer, a pathfinder. You open new possibilities, new territories, new continents, so that others can follow."[3]

This is the way for any relationship (business, home, church, politics) to become most meaningful and productive for all parties involved. But in our context, perhaps the most significant application has to do with helping your friend (and yourself, as well) learn to trust God. From the moment you first gaze out over that uncharted wilderness of heartbreak – knowing you need to help your friend cross it – to the times you're camped out together in the midst of that wasteland, surrounded by wild animals and other threatening forces, you may often wonder if you have made some grave error in judgment to have started this journey in the first place. You certainly don't feel much like a pathfinder at times like that.

Thankfully, as Covey points out, when synergy is operating, "the whole is greater than the sum of its parts. One plus one equals three or more."

Human synergy is a remarkable thing. We need each other. We draw upon each other. We can help each other, as we share this journey we call life. But how much more encouraging it is to know that as believers traverse the wilderness, one plus one *always* equals three because the Lord will never leave us or forsake us.

The biblical passage that perhaps best summarizes this is Ecclesiastes 4:9-12:

> Two are better than one, because they have a good return for their work:
> If one falls down, his friend can help him up.
> But pity the man who falls and has no one to help him up!
> Also, if two lie down together, they will keep warm.
> But how can one keep warm alone?

Though one may be overpowered, two can defend themselves.
A cord of three strands is not quickly broken.

In this case, the three-stranded cord is you, your friend, and
God! As you journey with your friend through the wasteland
called brokenness, you go together where neither of you would
have the security or courage to go alone, because what you are
together is more than either of you could possibly be alone.

And as you go, a curious thing can happen. Instead of always being exhausted from constantly giving and never receiving, you may discover that *through giving you have been receiving*. You may even feel energized and renewed. This is a work
of the Spirit of God.

On the other hand, as you help your friend, there may be
moments when the physical, mental, or spiritual depletion is
nearly overwhelming, because you have been willing to love
them enough to enter and share the pain. It is possible, if
you're not careful, that this depletion could take you toward
what's commonly called "burnout." But it's not inevitable, as
should be obvious when you witness some people—as Mother
Teresa—who seem to be able to give and give, and then give
some more. The key to maintaining, even increasing, your ability to help others is related to the last habit, and perhaps the
most important one.

Habit #7: Sharpen the Saw

If you're going to cut down a forest of trees, you need to
stop and sharpen your saw when it gets dull—or, if you're wise
enough, *before it gets dull*. The same principle applies to helping
others recover from loss. Renewal, a lifelong process, is more
than a spiritual issue. Just as depletion can involve body, soul
and spirit, renewing those personal resources—or keeping them
full—is crucial if you are going to avoid becoming a casualty
among many others who have tried to help their brokenhearted
friends.

How to Help a Heartbroken Friend

Here are a few components of health (see Covey's section on renewal for a more extensive analysis):

- Physical health requires eating right, getting sufficient rest and relaxation and exercising on a regular basis.
- Emotional health springs from an inner serenity (peace) that comes from having resolved the need to prove yourself or make something of yourself – as a result you will be relatively free from anxiety and depression and relatively happy and satisfied.
- Social health includes open, honest communication with others with whom you enjoy synergistic rather than adversarial relationships. Because you don't need to elevate yourself at the expense of others, or compete with them to achieve superiority, you are free to accept and affirm others (in other words, treat them with grace) while remaining committed to their best interests as their servant-friend.
- Your mind's health involves reading, reflecting, organizing, planning and working hard to communicate your thoughts coherently so that others will be challenged and blessed. Often this includes the "social" aspect of sharpening your thinking in the context of a group, or at least talking things through with one or more other persons, for "iron sharpens iron," as the Scripture says.
- The health of your own spirit is at its core a function of the depth of your experiential (versus theoretical or primarily intellectual) knowledge of and love for God. This relationship is really the key to living, now and into eternity. The acceptance that comes from God on the basis of your faith in Christ is the reason you have nothing to prove. The renewal of your mind that comes from pursuing Truth with the Spirit's help inspires your creative thinking. A deep appreciation for what God has done for you in Christ Jesus drives you to do his will, which is a primary reason you have embraced the ministry of reconciliation in the first place.

These are all factors in the lifelong process of becoming a whole person. Although, in a certain sense, believers are whole already, in the mind of God—who sees the perfection of Christ when he looks at Christ's brothers and sisters—there's also a not-yet aspect to the walk of faith. This is one reason we, and our friends, struggle so much with situations that bring us pain. We simply cannot respond supernaturally in every circumstance because we are not supernatural, nor are we yet perfectly conformed to the image of Jesus.

We long for that day when we will be like the Lord, for we shall see Jesus as he is, but now as we walk this sometimes difficult, confusing and painful path, we occasionally glimpse—as the disciples did on the way to Emmaus that first Easter afternoon—what it will be like to walk and talk with Christ forever. If you're like me, you're looking forward to understanding how the things that have so broken us (and our friends) were all tools in the hands of a Divine Sculptor who was chipping away the things in us that didn't look like God's Son.

In the meantime, the best we can do is to keep walking, trusting that one day God will make it all clear. As we walk, whether we're trying to help someone else or simply completing the journey set before us, the attitude that will keep us constantly renewed is that of a learner—or to use a synonym—a *disciple*, a student of Jesus Christ.

We cannot really help others unless this attitude is our guiding principle. For, as the Lord once said, "Can a blind person guide a blind person? Will not both fall into a pit? A disciple is not above the teacher, but everyone who is fully qualified will be like the teacher" (Lk 6:39-40).

As you and I complete the journey represented by this book, I want to make it clear that this disciple is not yet fully trained by the Master. But I'm not as blind as I once was and I do know where some of the pitfalls lie.

My hope is that by internalizing whatever is true, right, honorable and worthy of emulation in all I've shared—while

How to Help a Heartbroken Friend

ignoring the rest – you will be better equipped to complete your own pilgrimage with heartbreak, whether your friend's or your own.

I wish, as I come to the end of this book, that I could echo the thoughts of the apostle Paul, "Follow my example, as I follow the example of Christ" (1 Cor 11:1), but I still feel like I'm in Discipleship 101 at the University of Brokenness, so your best choice will be to follow Christ. That way, you can't go wrong, nor can you get lost, in your journey toward the wholeness that only knowing Christ can bring.

For Reflection or Discussion

1. If you learned that your friend's mother was in the ICU as the result of a heart attack and not expected to live through the night, how would you respond "proactively?" Why is this so important?

2. Have you ever been in a stressful situation where you were torn between calling for help and the prospect of having more stress introduced by another person's being around? Describe the experience, focusing on the feelings. How might this impact the way that you approach a person with a similar need?

3. Describe the conversation you projected a year from now between your heartbroken friend and yourself. Based on that exercise of imagination, in a group setting create a verbal thumbnail sketch of what recovery from heartbreak "looks like."

4. One of the signposts along the way of recovery is when grieving people begin to feel they don't want to stay where they are anymore. How could you tell that your friend has reached this point? What would you do to capitalize on this change and help them move in a constructive direction?

5. List the differences between pushing and leading someone on the path toward wholeness.

6. Contrast helping relationships that foster dependence, independence and interdependence. List the characteristics of each and then discuss how helping styles sometimes have to be flexible, based on the needs of the heartbroken person.

7. Why is it sometimes hard simply to observe while our friends engage in the inevitable wrestling match with God that comes with recovery from loss?

__ I wish I could protect them.

__ I'm afraid for their spiritual safety.

__ It reminds me too much of my own unresolved issues.

__ It's frustrating when I know how my friend should choose.

__ I'm not sure it is inevitable.

8. Can theologies (or denominational dogma) be coercive to persons in pain? If you sensed that this was happening to someone you were trying to help, how would you handle it? In a group setting, if several people in the group have experienced pressure of this sort, have them do a role play and then discuss it together, especially focusing on how to manage the different forces at work creatively.

9. What agendas might prevent your friend (and you) from discovering through your shared journey all that God has in mind?

10. How is the hypothetical visit to the optometrist in which the doctor hands the patient their own glasses – because they work for the doctor – similar to the way heartbroken Christians are sometimes treated? Have you ever been handled in this way? If so, how did it feel? How helpful was the advice (treatment) you received? What might you have said in response? What guiding principle can you see here in terms of how to help somebody else?

How to Help a Heartbroken Friend

11. Mutual discovery of what God is revealing is a major theme of this final chapter. How does asking rhetorical questions hinder this process?

12. Dr. Covey says that pathfinders or trailblazers must leave the security of base camp to confront an entirely new and unknown wilderness. What parallels can you think of in terms of the challenges of helping a heartbroken friend? Despite the difficulties of this approach, what are the potential benefits – to both you and your friend?

13. Discuss and further develop your own list of components of health. Rate yourself in each category, then write out a personal improvement plan for the next one month, six months, and one year. In a group setting, share as much or as little of this exercise as you wish with your group.

14. If you sometimes struggle with the tension between the "already" and the "not yet" aspects of faith, share how you try to approach this. What impact does this tension have on the degree to which we struggle with heartbreak – our own or someone else's? Is there a hidden benefit to this struggle, even though it does represent human weakness?

15. Compare the components of love from 1 Corinthians 13:4-8 with "the seven habits" of highly effective comforters as described in this chapter. Of the list of habits, what would you add, change or delete? What areas do you need most to work on and what specifically do you intend to do in relation to each?

16. If you've been working through this study in a group setting, take a few moments at the end of your final session to give a "word gift" to another member of your group, especially designed to address some need that person has expressed. You can do this verbally, but it might be less embarrassing and it might avoid the possibility of someone's being left out if you use the "card" method instead.

The card method: Have each member of the group write their name on the front of a three-by-five card at the beginning of the meeting, after which these are placed in a container and redistributed, one card to each, so that each participant has one person to think about and give a gift to (by writing it on the reverse side of the card) at the end of the meeting. (Anyone who draws their own name should take another card.)

At the end of the session, collect the completed cards, then distribute them by name and have the recipient read what has been written. Then close with prayer.

Notes

Chapter 8: Somebody to Hold Me

1. George Nichols, "It's Not Hard to Prevent Suicide," *Journal of the Christian Medical and Dental Society*, Volume XXI, No. 1, Spring 1990, pp. 10-12. Used by permission.

Chapter 9: To Tell the Truth

1. Erwin P. Rudolph, *John Bunyan and Pilgrim's Progress* (Wheaton: Victor Books, 1977), p. 63.
2. Ibid., p. 62.

Chapter 12: Seven Habits of Highly Effective Comforters

1. Stephen R. Covey, *The 7 Habits of Highly Effective People* (New York: Simon & Schuster, 1989), p. 201.
2. Ibid., pp. 262-263.
3. Ibid., pp. 263.

Additional copies of this book may be obtained
from your bookstore
or by contacting
Hope Publishing House
P.O. Box 60008
Pasadena, CA 91116 - U.S.A.
(626) 792-6123 / (800) 326-2671
Fax (626) 792-2121
E-mail: hopepub@sbcglobal.net
www.hope-pub.com